KRAFTWERK

MAN, MACHINE
and
MUSIC

by
Pascal Bussy

SAF Publishing Ltd

First published in 1993 by SAF Publishing Ltd.
Reprinted 1993, 1997

SAF Publishing Ltd.
12 Conway Gardens,
Wembley, Middx.
HA9 8TR
ENGLAND
TEL: 0181 904 6263
FAX: 0181 930 8565

In some cases it has not proved possible to ascertain or trace original illustration copyright holders, and the publishers would be grateful to hear from the photographers concerned.

ISBN 0 946719 09 8

Printed in England by Redwood Books, Trowbridge, Wiltshire.

KRAFTWERK

MAN, MACHINE
and
MUSIC

Interviews,
writing,
research
and
telephone calls:
PASCAL BUSSY

Additional writing,
research,
editing
and
home computing:
MICK FISH

THANKS
and
ACKNOWLEDGEMENTS

Thanks go primarily to Ralf Hütter and Florian Schneider for agreeing to be interviewed exclusively for this book.

We are also greatly indebted to former Kraftwerk member Karl Bartos and collaborators/advisors Emil Schult and Maxime Schmitt for their time, patience, verbal and visual contributions.

Thanks also for their incisive thoughts and recollections to (in alphabetical order):
Paul Alessandrini, Rebecca Allen, Patrick Codenys, Krista Fast, Martin Fraudreau, Michael Karoli, Kuêlan, Dan Lacksman, Didier Lestrade, Catherine McGill, William Orbit, Michael Rother, Irmin Schmidt, Marc Zermati.

Thanks also to: Masanori Akashi, Jean-Marc Bakouch, Olivier Bas, Jean-François Bizot, François Branchon, Ian Calder, Dominique Chelufour, Martin Cobb, Olivier Chanut (EMI France), Assaad Debs, Marc Devaud, Petra Gehrmann, Bernard Gely, Sylvain Gire, Andy Hallbery, Peter Hallbery, The Kensington Hilton, Hôtel de Nice, Stefan Ingmann, Jean-Luc Marre, Matten and Wiechers, Andrea Petrini, Jérôme Rey, Stephen Sheehan, Oscar Smit, Jacques Stroweis, Noreen Sullivan, Marc Thonon, Boris Venzen, Paul Widger, Paul Wilkinson, Pascale Ysebaert.

A special thank you to Dave Hallbery for design, layout and content advice.

CONTENTS

AUTHORS' NOTE

Writing a book about Kraftwerk was obviously going to be an uphill task. The group rarely give interviews, much less talk about their past. We started with an almost blank sheet of paper – assisted only by a love of their music, a few press clippings and a desire to find out more. On closer inspection most of the articles covered the same ground, but often with alarming discrepencies in detail.

Where to turn next? After all, it is a well documented fact that the group never answers correspondence. The kind of detective hunt that ensued was more like trying to penetrate the corridors of a secret society or intensely private business corporation than that of a pop group. Our research took on the appearance of a police-type investigation, each new lead giving us another name or telephone number. A common problem that we kept coming up against was that people were reluctant to talk to us without first having approval from the group.

As quite often happens when anything is clouded in secrecy and silence; rumours, stories and myths tend to multiply like a virus. This was an unavoidable problem in writing a book about a group who have chosen to cloak themselves in just such secrecy, not to mention complex imagery.

In compiling this book we have tried hard to avoid rumours and to stick as closely as possible to historical fact. However, we have based certain assumptions on articles about the group, which in themselves may have been partially inaccurate. Suffice to say, we have made every effort to check sources and verify stories, but inevitably some remain uncorroborated. Even so, perhaps now at the very least all the various facts and rumours about Kraftwerk are assembled in one place.

During our research, it soon became evident that those musicians who have been influenced by Kraftwerk were too numerous to even list, let alone interview. In view of this, we have concentrated on interviewing those who have actually met or worked with the group. Other than that we have let Kraftwerk's influence speak for itself by setting their story within the context of the development of electronic music.

Ultimately however, we must stress that this is not an official biography. Apart from the direct interview material, all the appraisal of Kraftwerk's music and image are the opinions of the authors and not necessarily how the various group members see themselves. We hope by analytically documenting their varied and elusive career we have in some ways enhanced awareness of one of the most fascinatingly beguiling and influential music groups of all time.

Pascal Bussy and Mick Fish – Paris, 1993.

FOREWORD

We are at the beginning of the 21st Century, Ralf Hütter and Florian Schneider are cycling in the Alps. Suddenly, they stop on a mountain pass. They take out of their pockets the miniaturised computers that they have with them. Into these computers they enter in special codes which launch simultaneous concerts in London, Madrid, Paris, Berlin, Moscow, Amsterdam, Rome and Stockholm. In each of these cities a group of pre-programmed robots is playing the music of Kraftwerk. In a few hours it will be New York, Montreal, and later on Los Angeles. The Tokyo and Sydney concerts are already finished.

On a small portable screen the two cyclists receive a message from their Düsseldorf Kling Klang studio where a team of engineers is controlling everything through a satellite connection: "alles OK" flickers on the screen. Ralf Hütter and Florian Schneider smile at each other and carry on cycling.

GERMANY
and
THE AVANT-GARDE

IN THE CENTRE OF DÜSSELDORF IS LOCATED ONE OF THE MOST UNIQUE and mysterious recording studios in the history of modern pop music. Although it houses banks of the most up-to-date recording technology and equipment, it has never been hired out and neither do its walls echo to stories of famous recording sessions by visiting pop musicians. This studio stands in an anonymous looking street, inside a yellowish building, overlooking a cheapish hotel with a Turkish grocery store nearby. The studio has no reception, no phone and accepts no mail. Unlike Abbey Road or the Sun Studios in Memphis, which receive hordes of interested tourists, this studio remains mostly unrecognised, having rarely been visited by music journalists, let alone the public. Nevertheless, some of the most innovative and startling records of the recent past have been recorded from within its confines. The place's name is the Kling Klang studio and for over 20 years it has been the workplace of one group – Kraftwerk.

For the duration of its existence, two musicians, Ralf Hütter and Florian Schneider, have met at this studio as an everyday routine – they have improvised, worked and meticulously recorded for posterity their vision of the world. It is a vision that could be loosely described as the quest for a type of sonic perfection – the constant striving for a new sound. In this quest, they have been joined by a limited and select group of musicians and engineers, as well as inanimate dummies and robots – all of whom have contributed in some way to make up the public product which is Kraftwerk.

From within the self-imposed seclusion of the Kling Klang studio they have created a factory-like environment – a laboratory where the musicians appear to work more like scientists than artists. This little home industry has consistently grown in stature if not in size and has embraced every new advancement in instrument technology, allowing each new machine to assume a life of its own. The sum total of their endeavours has the outward appearance of a streamlined, corporate business where the studio, the music and the image, have been manipulated into one unique entity vastly different from a run-of-the-mill pop group.

Yet this is a company which releases very little product – its workers are increasingly silent and uncommunicative. Infrequent LPs punctuated by the odd live performance are all the public now gets to see of Kraftwerk. In an entertainment business saturated with groups craving attention, airplay and record sales, it is surprising that the public hasn't lost interest in a group whose contact with the outside world is so minimal.

Exactly the opposite is the case. Kraftwerk are one of the most respected, revered, influential and namedropped groups of all time. Even more than that, it is now inconceivable to view the course of modern music without that piece of the jigsaw that is Kraftwerk. It is also impossible to see how such diverse groups as OMD and Depeche Mode through to Afrika Bambaataa and numerous house and techno exponents could exist in the form they do today without the influence of Kraftwerk. They have at one time or another been described as avant-garde musicians, creators of industrial music, founders of electronic pop, the Godfathers of techno music, even "The Beach Boys from Düsseldorf". The labels are endless and inevitably limiting, but all these tags are at least in some way appropriate.

Somehow, despite having existed for over 20 years, the group seem as modern today as they have always been. A remarkable and rare achievement in a world that thrives on the 'here today, gone tomorrow' ethic of a disposable pop culture. This is even more surprising considering that it has been achieved by a group who have had scant regard for any of the trends or niceties of the pop business, and are of a nationality not normally associated with much indigenous pop or rock music.

To trace the beginnings of what has become an institution and a total enigma within the music industry, it is necessary to look back to a period in the late sixties when rock and pop music was beginning to spread its wings across both musical and geographical boundaries. In fact, now that pop music is much more of a global business, it is easy to forget that there was a time when the idea of anything other than American or British rock music was almost inconceivable. Budding pop musicians from anywhere else in the world would inevitably look for inspiration to groups like The Beatles, The Rolling Stones or The Who in Britain – or Bob Dylan, The Beach Boys and The Doors in the US.

By 1967 the so-called "summer of love" was in full swing and a new spirit of experimentation saw certain rock musicians trying ever more daring excursions away from regimented forms of pop music. The atmosphere that allowed these musicians to surface was based around the slackening of attitudes, both social and musical, that had accompanied the emergence of the hippy movement. Many of pop music's leading lights had started to turn their backs on the singles-orientated pop market and had adopted a new, more experimental, album-orientated rock music. The influence of rhythm and blues that had dominated the music of The Beatles and The Stones was now being abandoned in favour of more open structures borrowed from free-form jazz and ethnic music, often fuelled by copious quantities of LSD.

In England, Pink Floyd and The Soft Machine were not only pioneers of a new fusion of music but also participants in large multi-media events, love-ins or happenings that far exceeded the expectations of an average rock concert. At the same time, on the West Coast of America groups like the Grateful Dead, Jefferson Airplane and Frank Zappa and the Mothers of Invention were headlining their own cosmic acid-marathons with a strange mixture of totally spontaneous improvisation, feedback and traditional American music. Similarly in New York, as an antidote to all the peace and love of the West Coast scene, The Velvet Underground, under the guiding hand of Andy Warhol, were staging their own multi-media events based around the group's amphetamine-induced throbbing mantras and flashing light shows.

The hippy revolution and the notoriety surrounding the "happenings" soon spread from the USA and Britain to the youth of mainland Europe carrying with it more challenging ideas than mere loud rock music. Sexual and drug experimentation, the emerging prominence of the feminist, gay and peace movements, all culminated in the feeling that young people now had a more effective political voice for change.

However, in the main, Europeans like the French and Germans did not yet have their own indigenous rock groups. By and large, European efforts at producing contemporary music were considered laughable, confined to the sort of derivative hum-drum sing-a-long songs of the *Eurovision Song Contest.* Most European bands contented themselves by playing cover versions of their British or American mentors, mostly regurgitating rock music's now burgeoning thesaurus of cliches but with the lyrics sung in slightly foreign accents.

Perhaps because of the lack of musical role models, the European student movements took on serious political overtones. They were unwilling to merely sit around with flowers in their hair listening to rock music, thus avoiding the hedonistic excesses produced by the London, San Francisco and New York hippy 'scenes'.

The climax of this political activity occured in Paris in May 1968, in an outbreak of youth rebellion that saw widescale rioting by left-wing students in the French capital, the intense severity of which caught the authorities napping. The destabilising violence that ensued, in some ways outweighed that of the peace demos and anti-Vietnam War demonstrations in America and Britain, so much so that it nearly succeeded in bringing down the French Government. Here was an anarchic display of disorder that was far broader in its political agenda than even that of the more radical hippies.

In Germany too, changing destinies reflected a deeper sense of political youth commitment. The country was still afflicted by a "cold war" menace fuelled by tensions between East and West. Consequently, a new generation of young West Germans were wrestling with a consciousness that remained in the shadows of Nazism and the Second World War, even though they were too young to have actually experienced the holocaust.

It was from within this political instability that a number of German artists like Beuys, Richter and Kiefer started to explore ways of recapturing a German cultural identity. Similarly, a new world of opportunities opened up to film students like Fassbinder and Wenders. Also, a whole bunch of avant-garde music students became interested in challenging mainstream ideas about what constituted music. Of all the German groups that emerged on the crest of this particular experimental wave, three in particular – Can, Tangerine Dream and Kraftwerk – would go on to have a lasting influence on the international music scene.

The primary group to make an impact were Can. Formed in Cologne in 1968, their influence would dominate German music for a decade. Somehow, Can managed to inject into their music a passion and anarchy that mirrored the student riots of 1968. They quickly became popular in Germany, Britain and France, where their mixture of quirky improvisation and ethnic influences was most readily appreciated.

Can's music was constructed in their own self-appointed studio, a room in a castle called Schloss Norvenich. Immersing themselves for days on end, they worked on pieces through a process of extensive improvisation over a steady and repetitious drum beat. The effect was to create a trance-like music that seemed to be both wildly random whilst being strictly regimented and disciplined. Live, the group often played long sets that disregarded conventional song structures – songs were considered almost bourgeois. Now young people in Europe were getting a taste of their own homegrown 'happenings' similar to those going on in London, San Francisco and New York.

Can's initial impetus was as much born out of the classical avant-garde as it was contemporary rock music – two of the group, Irmin Schmidt and Holger Czukay, having studied classical composition under Karlheinz Stockhausen. However, although most of Can were classically trained, they were never overly concerned with the symphonic pretensions that were captivating their British counterparts from classical backgrounds like Emerson, Lake & Palmer and Yes.

The real long-lasting influence of Can on subsequent German bands lay in their emphasis on rhythmic repetition. Jaki Liebezeit played with metronomic precision, and remains one of the most influential and respected drummers in rock music. At a time when most drummers were showing an unrestrained flamboyance typified by Carl Palmer, Liebezeit was honing his technique to an absolute minimum, providing a solid base for the improvisational layers of sound produced by the rest of the group.

Can succeeded in building a bridge between the rarified atmosphere of the classical avant-garde and the more traditional approach of rock music. Once they had started the ball rolling by expanding musical barriers, other German music students took up the mantle, using the newest developments in instrument technology. In the years that followed, a whole gaggle of German groups attracted a sizeable fringe following across Europe and were tagged, somewhat derogatorily, by the UK music press as 'Kraut Rock'. However, the very existence of the tag signified for the first time it was possible to look outside the boundaries of the UK and the USA for a source of innovation in rock music.

Probably the major early influence on the perception of German synthesizer music were Tangerine Dream. "The Tangs" as they became affectionately known, had been formed in 1967 by a trained artist and sculptor, Edgar Froese, together with Klaus Schulze and Conrad Schnitzler. Froese had spent some time in the mid-sixties in Cadaques with Salvador Dali, whilst Schnitzler went under the rather splendid nickname of "the mad genius from Berlin". The group were initially a traditional rock band, but mainly under Schnitzler's influence they became a totally electronic synthesizer band.

Later on, Tangerine Dream's ambient synthesized music throbbed with a similar trance-like repetition to that of the music of Can. With little percussive element to speak of (drum machines not being widely available then), the rhythm was provided by the repetitive pulses and wave signals produced by the synthesizer. This was particularly evident in the repeated arpeggios that provided a rhythmic track of their own. Here was a totally new underground form of music that by its nature ignored the very idea of singles. The length of the pieces (often exceeding 20 minutes) meant that they stood little chance of being played on the radio.

Soon Can and Tangerine Dream were joined by a proliferation of other German groups like Amon Düül, Ash Ra Tempel, Guru Guru,

Faust and Cluster, all of whom seemed to have little regard for the niceties or cliches of rock 'n' roll. They preferred to extend the boundaries of the perceived confines of "music". Unlike many jazz or classical avant-garde musicians who may have had broadly the same aims, these German groups were guided by a mischievous anarchic spirit. As a result they managed to avoid becoming marginalised, aiming their music toward mainstream rock audiences.

However, it soon became evident that there were further steps to take if this new German music was to make a lasting impact. Can, and especially Amon Düül, were connected with a 'hippyish' and anarchic imagery, being associated with the sixties and the so-called drug culture. Similarly, although the music of Tangerine Dream had all the elements of modern technology, their image was still that of rather dowdy looking university professor-types playing with synthesizers. At this juncture 'Kraut Rock' could easily have ended up as a historical curio, a musical cul-de-sac that had been tacked onto the late '60s and early '70s hippy scene, with a limited if potent influence.

Even so, Can and Tangerine Dream were rewarded by quick success – not to mention a certain degree of notoriety. (A famous 1974 concert by Tangerine Dream and Nico in Rheims Cathedral led to calls from the Pope for the building to be resanctified). As well as disapproval from the Vatican, the rock establishment were beginning to show signs of recognition to the point where German rock music could no longer be viewed as a joke. This increased awareness created the framework for the third, arguably most influential, and certainly the most commercially successful German group to flourish.

Kraftwerk, having arisen out of this experimental explosion, moved the whole perception of German music up a gear, ultimately extending the experimental philosophy and shining a torch toward a more technologically motivated future. These new obsessions were taken to their logical conclusion, finally establishing synthesizer music with mass-market credibility. Spawning legions of imitators and influencing music far beyond the experimental or electronic, they were to provide the natural link between the German avant-garde scene and electronic pop music.

However, this was a slow and metamorphic process. When two classically trained musicians – Ralf Hütter and Florian

Schneider-Esleben – first met at the Kunstakademie (Academy of Arts) in Remschied, near Düsseldorf, they could have had little idea of what the future held in store. Like Can and Tangerine Dream, they were just students whose dream was to play music that expanded upon conventional notions rather than merely copying British and American rock music.

Ralf Hütter was born in the town of Krefeld, near Düsseldorf, on 20th August, 1946. The son of a doctor, Hütter now describes his upbringing as "normal, devoid of interest. Nothing special."[1] As the main spokesman for the group, this is typical of the sort of laconic response he gives to questions about their private lives – lives which they have consistently claimed as being normal and boring.

Today, Hütter is equally as cagey about his early influences, now describing his first musical memories as, "nothing... Silence."[2] He admits to having listened to the radio but adds that it was, "nothing exciting. No memory about that. No flash, no event, no shock."[3] This type of memory lapse conveniently camouflages Hütter's life outside of the group. However, strangely for someone who now claims his early musical interests were nothing and silence, Hütter did actually spend a number of years studying classical piano from which he gathered enough musical impetus to study electric organ at the Düsseldorf Conservatory. It was in the improvising class that he met up with the distinctive looking Florian Schneider-Esleben.

Florian Schneider was born on April 7th, 1947, in a small town in the Bodensee area in the South of Germany, near the Swiss and Austrian borders. When Florian was three, the Schneider family moved to Düsseldorf, where he lived with his father Paul Schneider, his mother Eva Maria Esleben, and his two sisters. Florian's father was a well-known architect, being responsible for a number of notable design projects in Germany including railway stations and airports. One his most famous designs was the Haniel-Garage in Düsseldorf which was built in 1949. This unique building was a transparent glass, five-floor car park for 700 cars.

Düsseldorf itself was ravaged by bomb damage and bore the scars of war. Florian Schneider:

"Much of the town was still destroyed. I remember the streets were full of all these bomb holes, it was a bit like it is in the Lebanon now. But as a child this did not seem terrible at all, I had the feeling that the streets were a very exciting place to play, but of course it was very dangerous as well..."[4]

By the age of five, the young Florian had already been exposed to his parents' record collection, including such unusual recordings as the concrete musique of Pierre Henry. However, being brought up in the conflicting atmosphere of post-war Germany, the radio not only played late night electronic broadcasts of the sort that his parents would listen to, but also a lot of American music, as there was still a large allied troop presence in the town.

Schneider started by playing the recorder and, encouraged by his mother, soon moved on to the flute, even playing in some local jazz combos. It was music, and in particular the flute, that Schneider went on to study at the Düsseldorf Conservatory. Florian Schneider:

"I studied seriously up to a certain level, then I found it boring, I looked for other things, I found that the flute was too limiting... Soon I bought a microphone, then loudspeakers, then an echo, then a synthesizer. Much later I threw the flute away, it was a sort of process."[5]

At the Conservatory, Hütter and Schneider became inseparable friends and found that they not only came from similar backgrounds, but also shared an interest in improvised avant-garde music. Like many early improvisers, their initial musical attempts were much more experimental than tuneful. Hütter explains, "the idea was to make contemporary electronic music."[6] However, as such, the duo had no defined musical plan. Ralf Hütter:

"We didn't really have a strategy, we rushed into making industrial music, abandoning all our other activities from before – our education, our classical background. It was a total rupture for us. Neither then nor now did we think about the future, or about some strategy. Why would we think about the future?"[7]

Although having no decisive musical plan, or acknowledging any particular early influences, their initial musical experiments were generally similar in both form and inspiration to their compatriots Can and Amon Düül. Just how aware or influenced by each other these groups were remains very much a matter of conjecture, although the marked similarity in musical content would tend to lead to the conclusion that they at least shared some sort of common spirit without necessarily feeling part of a movement as such. Certainly much of this apparent cohesion must be put down to the similarity in classical background which meant they were exposed to the same kind of avant-garde music.

One of the most notable influences on all the early German rock groups was the central figure of Karlheinz Stockhausen. As leader of the Darmstadt school, his influence on the electronic music field was immense. His experiments with electronic sounds were also influential on rock musicians further afield – his picture being one of those included on the cover of The Beatles' *Sgt. Pepper* LP. Incidentally, Hütter told the journalist Jean-Francois Bizot that he and Schneider had been to see a Stockhausen concert in Cologne in the late '60s having taken LSD beforehand. Whether this would have helped or hindered making sense of Stockhausen's music is debatable. His theories were concerned with expanding musical environments, being rather pretensiously described as "continuous event concerts in non-specific buildings" and often featured what appeared to be random blasts of sound.

Similarly influential was the Italian composer Russolo who built up what was described as "musique bruitiste" with noises and sound effects. Also, the Fluxus group (among them LaMonte Young, Jon Hassell and Tony Conrad) from New York were constant visitors to Germany. Conrad even went on to record an album in the '70s with the German band Faust. The last component that made up this avant-garde jigsaw was the considerable interaction between the French Radio station France Musique – where composer Pierre Schaeffer played a huge role as a radio pioneer – and its equivalent radio stations in Germany.

All these influences were in some way responsible for shaping the emerging electronic rock scene in Germany. Contrary to Hütter's current assertions as to having no early influences as such, it is most probable that both he and Schneider were as affected by this creative nucleus of experimental music as the other German musicians starting out at the same time.

Certainly by 1968, Hütter and Schneider had already begun to put their improvising experiments to some use. They formed the core of a group called Organisation whose early music was a mixture of feedback, sounds and rhythm. As music students, they could have chosen to work in any number of different fields, but they consciously chose to interpret their early improvisation within the bounds of a rock band. Group friend and journalist Paul Alessandrini:

"The interesting thing is that both of them came from families of the upper middle class. Sometimes I get the feeling that they were intellectuals from the high bourgeoisie who wanted to discover another world. They have always been fascinated by discoteques and girls, and coming from the sort of social background and education they did, music was the only way. They had this German aspect, the family aspect, very starchy – and they wanted to team up with the rock world."[8]

This immersion into the "rock world" meant that Organisation began taking part in various performances at universities and art galleries. However, this was a world which was vastly different from the trappings of rock 'n' roll in the UK or USA. Many of the German music students considered themselves less part of any rock scene, and more like performance artists who were making a musical art statement. Ralf Hütter:

"We were very lucky, at the time there were electronic music concerts, happenings, the Fluxus group etc. It was very normal, we played on the same circuit, the galleries. When we began we didn't have any engagements in the traditional music world, we were engaged in the artistic world, galleries, universities, etc."[9]

Michael Karoli of Can remembers one such multi-media event as being one of the first early connections between the two groups:

"The first time I remember meeting them was in the summer of 1968. I remember Ralf being very communicative, but Florian didn't speak so much. It was the time when they were involved with their band Organisation. Malcolm Mooney had just joined us and we were to play at the preview of a painting exhibition. We had not brought many instruments with us, so we played one long piece on their instruments for about 15 minutes. As far as I can remember this was Can's first public appearance.

Later, when they had formed Kraftwerk, they came to Schloss Norvenich four or five times and we played jam sessions together in the afternoons."[10]

Subsequently, Karoli contrasted the difference between the two groups, "Kraftwerk were very German. I think that we were more open."[11] Can's keyboard player Irmin Schmidt remembers that later on the two groups played a concert for the radio together, and that after that they would meet up for a drink from time to time. "Kraftwerk were the perfect antithesis of Can", but Schmidt adds, "I find their music as impersonal as it is original, but it is saved by its humorous side."[12]

Back in 1969 the experimental wave of German music had caused enough of a stir in their home country for many of the new groups to find outlets for their material through recording contracts. The result of this flurry of deals saw the release of Can's debut record *Monster Movie*, together with *Amon Düül* by Amon Düül I, and following a split in the group, *Phallus Dei* and *Yeti* by Amon Düül II.

The following year the momentum continued. Not only did Can release their hugely influential *Tago Mago* double LP, but there were also debut releases by other groups like Xhol Caravan, Embryo and Tangerine Dream. Not to be outdone, Organisation recorded an LP called *Tone Float* in early 1970. Initially recorded for Conny Plank's company Rainbow Productions, the music was produced and engineered by Conny Plank in his temporary studio which at the time was located in a disused refinery. Rainbow had been set up by Plank not only to record contemporary German rock bands, but also to act almost as an agency, providing business help to find a release for their material. As a result, when the LP was completed, Plank visited England and took it to a friend who had connections with RCA who were sufficiently impressed to release it as an LP.

Conrad (known to all as Conny) Plank was an amateur jazz musician who had become a radio sound technician. By the time he teamed up with Hütter and Schneider, Plank's pedigree was already established as he had worked as an apprentice to Wolfgang Hirschman who was renowned for doing the live sound for Marlene Dietrich. This had given Plank the unique opportunity of being the sound engineer on a Duke Ellington session.

Although loving all sorts of music, Plank had become interested in British and American rock music, and in particular, The Rolling Stones, Jimi Hendrix and The Velvet Underground. He also admired the simplicity of the music of the Jamaican producer Lee Perry and the minimal technology that was used to produce it. Perhaps more importantly he quickly realised that it was pointless for European musicians to try and imitate British or American groups, something which he hated, and as a producer set about devising ways of giving groups like Organisation a discernibly European identity and sound.

Despite having a specifically German outlook, Hütter and Schneider chose to operate under the English name of Organisation for their first LP. However, it was an unusually ambitious step for a German group to sign to an English label. This could have been interpreted as a potentially groundbreaking move, exposing German music to a wider English audience, but it was one which partially back-fired. English audiences were not quite ready for the new wave of German groups. Furthermore, as RCA was a British record company, the LP was only available in their native Germany as an import and thus failed to sell many copies.

The front cover featured a pseudo-mythological drawing by the mysteriously named Comus, of the sort that was fairly common place on LP sleeves in the early '70s. In attempting to be enigmatic it bore more than a passing resemblance to the cover of the first King Crimson LP but was much less successful as an image.

On the back cover was the first appearance of the duo's early adopted symbol – the soon to be familiar image of the traffic cone. In choosing an everyday mass-produced image, Hütter and Schneider had been influenced by the early sixties art of Andy Warhol. The traffic cone represented a similarly anonymous image to that of Warhol's "Campbell's Soup Cans" and "Coca-Cola Bottles". They were no doubt impressed by Warhol's knack of taking an object of little significance and turning it into a trademark. By adopting the symbol of the traffic cone they were making a similar artistic gesture. Whilst Warhol's "Coca-Cola Bottles" symbolised everyday Americana, the traffic cone was an everyday image that could be seen aplenty on the German autobahns.

On *Tone Float*, the Organisation line up consisted of Hütter on organ, Schneider on flute and violin, Basil Hammoudi on vocals, Butch Hauf on bass, and Fred Monicks on drums. Unlike conventional rock groups who have a body of songs ripened and honed by constant gigging and ready for inclusion on a debut LP, many experimental bands' first waxings verge on the tentative. The Organisation LP is no exception, and their initial step into recording, like much else in their somewhat elusive and blurred past, is something they are reticent to expand upon. Florian Schneider:

> "We were very young, and we were just trying different things. The group was me and Ralf, and some other people who changed from time to time. We were maybe the most important members, but both of us also worked on different projects. I don't remember so well..."[13]

The *Tone Float* LP elicits comparisons with many others who were experimenting with the fringes of feedback and noise at that time, such as the early Pink Floyd. Later in 1975, Lester Bangs asked Hütter if Kraftwerk felt a debt to Pink Floyd. "No", he replied, "It's vice versa. They draw from French classicism and German electronic music."[14]

It is easy to understand why Hütter would more readily want to acknowledge the classical avant-garde rather than any debt they owed to the early Pink Floyd who, by the time of Hütter's statement, had become rather unfashionable in the eyes of the critics. However, with *Tone Float*'s clumsy percussion, rather doom-laden bass lines and ponderous organ chords, comparisons with Pink Floyd are difficult to ignore.

Similarities with Can are also evident, but the title track "Tone Float", which takes up the whole of side one, and other tracks like "Silver Forest" and "Milk Rock", do not build in anywhere near as tense or dynamic a way as their improvising contemporaries. So, even though the Organisation LP has the same spontaneous feel, it lacked the direction or impetus of Can's powerful debut LP *Monster Movie*.

Tone Float's weird noises and percussive breaks are used in a rather haphazard way that has a certain quaint charm but no lasting potency. Somewhat similar to Pink Floyd's first post-Syd Barrett LP, *Ummagumma*, released a year earlier, the pieces all too often meander and irritate rather than intrigue. Whereas during its better moments *Ummagumma* relies on its melodic strengths, *Tone Float* has no such backbone to fall back on.

The LP features repetitive percussion and bass drum patterns, embellished with guitar, flute, violin and organ, all vying for attention. More often than not Hütter's organ playing dominates proceedings, but very much in the soloing mode of improvisation, presumably encouraged by classes at the Conservatory, showing none of the restraint that would dominate later LPs.

Sections of the music are clearly '60s influenced and have an almost eastern feeling with scratchy violin and bongos. On the whole they fail to achieve anywhere near the eery mantric feeling of The Velvet Underground or the cosmic humour of the early Floyd. But there are glimpses, however brief, of Hütter and Schneider's interest in minimalism as certain moments on the LP almost seem to peter out into silence.

The Organisation LP having been released through RCA, neither sold well nor made the impression that some of the other German groups had achieved. It was obvious that the duo would have to find not only a different record label, but also a more confident sound if they were to establish an identity of their own and emerge from the shadows cast by their more successful compatriots. However it is interesting, if nothing else, as an example of the growing pains of two musicians who were eventually to break out of the restrictions imposed on them by unstructured improvised music.

In reality, any comparison between the later Kraftwerk sound and the Organisation LP is hard to draw. It is quite easy to understand why Hütter and Schneider might later want to draw a quiet veil over this earliest part of their career. Certainly, *Tone Float* cannot conceivably be considered as the duo's forgotten masterpiece, in fact, many people remain unaware of the LP and assume that their first recording was the self-titled *Kraftwerk* that appeared in the autumn of the same year.

Tone Float was the last time that Hütter and Schneider would rely totally on the unrestrained free-form expression of an improvising band. Perhaps they realised that undisciplined improvisation could be as restricting as song structures. Also, with Organisation being essentially a democratic five piece band, it was difficult to develop a disciplined approach. When they were to record again a few months later, the duo could concentrate on a harder more regimented edge, and the seeds of the more familiar Kraftwerk sound would be much more apparent.

SOUND
and
INDUSTRY

BY MID-1970, MUCH OF THE NEWLY BORN GERMAN ROCK MUSIC tradition could be boiled down to two particularly German fascinations – technology and efficiency. Central to the appeal of 'Kraut Rock' was a music which, although initially anarchic and experimental, was nevertheless efficient in a minimally mesmeric way. Also intriguing was the harnessing and conquering of the latest technological breakthroughs in instrumentation. This resulted in musicians who were very technically minded, conscious of bridging the gap between musician and studio engineer. As an inevitable outcome, groups established their own recording studios or bases, which in themselves could be used as creative tools. Thus, the recording process was now perceived in a similar way to that of an artist or a sculptor approaching a painting or sculpture in his or her own studio.

This building-block approach was in stark contrast to most conventional pop and rock groups. British and US groups saw the recording process as one of writing a bunch of songs and then booking into a commercial studio for a few days or weeks to record them. Can, however, could now revel in the control afforded to them of their own recording studio – almost like having the benefits of a home industry or little factory where they could constantly work and refine their ideas. Perhaps, more importantly, the time taken in building up these ideas made it economically impractical to record in a fully commercial studio. As Hütter put it, "The studio was really born before the group. Everything came from the studio, as from a Mutterschiff (Mothership)."[1]

Can's somewhat eccentric bass player, Holger Czukay, became absorbed by the apparent dialogue that went on between himself and the recording machines in their Inner Space studio. Hütter and Schneider too, whilst lacking Czukay's mischievous edge, became intrigued by the notion of a new type of technological music. They started to entertain similar ideas to that of Czukay – that recording machines could assume a life of their own.

Later, of course, there was little distinction in Kraftwerk between the music and the studio. In effect, advances in recording technology would become the raison d'etre of the group's existence. Eventually, they became obsessed with producing music that almost sounded as if it had been created by machines – not just musicians who were also studio engineers, but more like sound engineers who happened to produce music. This led to the logical conclusion that the studio was a musical instrument or member of the group in its own right. As they would put it, "we play the studio". Ultimately, as the Kraftwerk sound developed, the studio became a kind of technical laboratory, claiming that they were not so much entertainers as scientists.

However, this could only have been a twinkling in their eye when Hütter and Schneider took the inevitable step early in 1970 of establishing their own makeshift studio in the centre of Düsseldorf. In the same building as it is today, it was set up in a 60 sq metre rented loft in close proximity to the main railway station. After fitting out the room with sound insulation material they started recording sounds on stereo tape machines and cassette recorders with a view to taking the tapes to a fully equipped recording studio for final mixing. It was even reported that part of this recording process involved the duo having microphones hidden in their clothing so as to capture various sounds as they moved around.

Düsseldorf being located in the industrial heartland of Germany provided Kraftwerk with the inspiration for many of these early tapes, recreating the sounds of the flat industrialized zone on the banks of the nearby Rhine. From very early on they were forging musical connections between the exterior world and their own interior idealised vision of that same world as constructed from within the confines of their studio. The studio acted like a musical filter for the sonic snapshots that Hütter and Schneider took from the industrial reality that surrounded them.

The musical development of Kraftwerk was inextricably linked with the small but thriving city of Düsseldorf. Located in the western region of Germany, hugging the Dutch border, it was the perfect place for the birth of the Kraftwerk musical ideology, being symbolic of a new German modernity after the Second World War. Just as Frankfurt had become the symbol of financial power, so Düsseldorf was the main city of the "Ruhrgebiet", the biggest industrial concentration in Europe. As such it symbolised a new form of industrial power represented by clean, modern design. In musical terms this was reflected in the differences between Can, who produced a more traditional music from the solid cultural background of Cologne, and Kraftwerk who were to go on to adopt a more modern musical language from their base in Düsseldorf.

After disbanding Organisation, the duo had adopted the name Kraftwerk (literally Power Plant). By choosing a specifically German name rather than an anglicized one, it was a clear statement of Germanic intent, as well as possibly claiming the higher ground over other popular German groups who had adopted English names. In fact, it was common practice for rock groups in Germany to choose names that reflected the sort of music they played, rather than picking a random or arbitrary one like many English and American rock bands. Therefore the word Can, having meaning in English, Turkish and Japanese reflected the ethnic interests of the group. Likewise, the names Ash Ra Tempel and Tangerine Dream reflected the more typically "cosmic" end of the German rock scene. Needless to say, the name Kraftwerk came to speak volumes about the industrial influence and motivation that Hütter and Schneider's new group would embrace.

However, according to the group's later collaborator Karl Bartos, the name was contrived from less intellectual beginnings. Apparently, Hütter and Schneider, on a trip to East Germany, had been amused by the names of football teams like Dynamo Dresden. They all seemed to have rather grand and industrial connections. Hütter and Schneider started playing around with imaginary team names of their own with prefixes like Kraftwerk, and thus the name stuck. An added attraction to the name Kraftwerk was that they would actually gain a lot of free advertising. On German roads the power stations (kraftwerks) are indicated by road signs. So, every 100 kms or so you would come across a sign that indicates to turn off to the kraftwerk. The group were very aware of this extra angle to the appeal of their name.

Not only did they choose a German name but all the early tracks that the group worked on had German titles as well. By not conforming and anglicizing their product, they were making a conscious effort, however small, to regain some of the ground that German culture had lost in the post-war years. They were trying to reverse the 'Americanisation' that had been imposed on many aspects of German society, and most particularly popular music. By being the first of the new German groups to title pieces exclusively in the German language, they were expressing themselves with an even stronger central European identity. Ralf Hütter:

"The culture of Central Europe was cut off in the thirties, and many of the intellectuals went to the USA or France, or they were eliminated. We [Kraftwerk] are picking it up again where it left off, continuing this culture of the thirties, and we are doing this spiritually."[2]

Hütter and Schneider were all too aware that there was a whole generation of Germans, aged between 30 and 50, who had lost their identity, both during the war and in the immediate post-war period. Many Germans referred to this period as "die Stunde null" (the hour zero) referring not only to the economy and politics, but also to culture and music. Perhaps more than any of the other German groups, Kraftwerk expressed through their music the rebuilding and continuing of Germany's past culture. Hütter later expanded on this to Lester Bangs in 1975.

"So you see another group like Tangerine Dream, although they are German they have an English name, so they create onstage an Anglo-American identity, which we completely deny. We want the whole world to know we are from Germany, because the German mentality, which is more advanced, will always be part of our behaviour. We create out of the German language, the mother language, which is very mechanical, we use it as the basic structure of our music."[3]

It would be all too easy to attribute right-wing overtones to this statement with its talk of an "advanced mentality" and "mother language". In reality Kraftwerk have always appeared politically ambivalent, and such answers must be taken on an artistic and cultural level rather than in a political context. However, in expressing their national identity in such a way, they may have been reacting against the hippyish, more left-wing orientation of most of the other German groups whom Kraftwerk had largely outgrown by the time of Hütter's statement.

Back in 1970, following the mutual disappointment between the group and RCA over the lack of success of *Tone Float*, Hütter and Schneider started to look for a record company with German connections to release their next record. They ended up signing a deal with the newly established Philips label. The label was owned by the Hamburg-based Phonogram, itself a subsidiary of the Dutch parent company Philips, who had strong links with the large German company Siemens AG. In a rather roundabout way, it somehow seemed harmonious for the burgeoning pioneers of a modern industrial music to be connected with one of the top industrial companies in Germany. Kraftwerk were only the third signing to Philips, after the now forgotten Ihre Kinder in 1969, and Frumpy in 1970. At the time most of the other German groups were either on United Artists' subsidiary Liberty, like Can and Amon Düül, or like most of the Berlin bands on Metronome's subsidiaries Brain, Ohr and Pilz.

The first fruit of their signing to Philips was the self-titled *Kraftwerk* LP. Recorded between July and August of 1970 in their new studio, it was co-produced and engineered by Conny Plank, this time with the assistance of Klaus Löhmer. Plank, by then an experienced engineer, could presumably have chosen to concentrate on more lucrative work. However, because he believed so strongly in the pioneering music of Kraftwerk, he helped with the recording process often for little or no remuneration. His was a key role, being crucial in developing Hütter and Schneider's recording abilities up to the point where they could perceive themselves more as studio engineers than musicians.

Like most good producers Plank was good at organising people within a studio environment. He felt that the best music was made when musicians and producers "play together like children play together."[4] Plank was later to describe the early Kraftwerk sessions as very long, with everybody hanging around, sometimes not doing much at all. Then someone would make a few suggestions and one of the group would decide whether they liked it or not. From Plank's description it was clear that even this early on, with limited time constraints, the Kraftwerk creative process could be a slow one. As Plank put it, "To me it is more important that the picture is right no matter what sounds are used on tape."[5]

When released in late 1970, as a point of continuity from the Organisation LP, *Kraftwerk*'s double opening LP sleeve was designed by Hütter and showcased their adopted trademark – the traffic cone. Both front and back covers featured a dayglo orange and white traffic cone with the word Kraftwerk overprinted. For the uninitiated, it was not clear whether one was to assume that this was the name of the LP or the band, or both. Opening the double sleeve of the album revealed a large photo of an electric generator, another indicator of the industrial and technological image that the group was beginning to embrace.

From the very opening notes of the LP, it is evident that the duo had quickly put much of the meandering uncertainties of *Tone Float* behind them, arriving at a much more disciplined form of music. *Kraftwerk* contained a lot of the elements that would later make up the group's sound, without ever perhaps making a conclusive whole. Rhythmically it is much stronger, featuring Andreas Hohman and Klaus Dinger on drums. Initially they had difficulty in finding drummers who could embrace their more avant-garde ideas. Ralf Hütter:

> "Not only were we interested in Musique Concrete but also in playing organ tone clusters and flute feedback sounds that added variety to the repeated note sequences that we recorded and mixed on tape. Then we used several acoustic drummers as we turned our attention to more rhythmic music, and soon found that amplifying drums with contact mics was desirable for us but not readily accepted by the players."[6]

As a result of the difficulty in getting drummers to adapt to their music, the LP also features Florian Schneider on electronic percussion. This was undoubtedly the result of Schneider's early efforts at building homemade rhythm devices on which he would later so successfully modify and expand. However, in choosing Hohman and Dinger they were obviously aware of bringing in two people who were naturally rhythmically inclined, providing a balance in the group between rhythm and experimentation. It also gave more of an impression of a working band of four members, even if all the other instrumentation and compositions were credited to Hütter and Schneider.

Side one opens with "Ruckzuck", a piece which was to become a live favourite of the group. They often started their early concerts with this track which is dominated by Schneider's breathy flute riff. Following on is the 12 minute "Stratovarius" which, although having an eery improvised feel, gives the impression that the structure of the piece is altogether more ordered. The types of sound are more subtle and the track builds with an inner momentum and logic. The title of the track is a play on words possibly alluding toward classical music as subject matter (i.e. Stradivarius). The tempo speeds up and slows down to various climaxes, ending with a plaintive violin and flute played over a minimal percussive beat. The final climax ends suddenly and abruptly like someone has turned the volume off.

Side two opens with "Megaherz" which begins with a low oscillating note slowly developing into waves of industrial sound. This finally gives way to a quiet passage which has an almost classically minimal tune, showing an early understanding of the sort of basic melody lines they were later to use to such effect.

However, some of the music on *Kraftwerk* still bore more than a passing similarity to their German contemporaries. "Stratovarius" has the same percussive climaxes as Can, whilst passages in "Megaherz" have a similar ambient, cathedral-like quality to the music of Tangerine Dream. But it is the LP's last track which really begins to state the group's forthcoming electronic agenda. On "Vom Himmel Hoch", noise swoops from speaker to speaker, tension building as stabs of industrial sound are joined by a tribal drum beat. Some passages sound like machines that have been left to their own devices, bleeping and twitching like radios and amplifiers feeding-back in a corner. The intensity and probable direction of the duo was now clear as the track steps out of the shadows of their contemporaries as a menacingly evocative portrayal of industrial sound.

Compared to the Organisation LP, *Kraftwerk* was a considerable artistic success. They had managed to mix a blend of obsessional rhythms, flute whispers, organ sighs and treated violin sounds, giving a much stronger almost hallucenogenic effect. Sounds glide in and out, monotonous and hypnotic rhythms build only to disappear. Similar to pieces by Terry Riley and Steve Reich, childish, almost nursery rhyme melodies, evolve and slightly change over the course of a track.

With a successful recording under their belts, the group's confidence had grown to such an extent that they were able to consider playing more concerts in their native Germany. These concerts were often advertised with a poster featuring the red and white traffic cone with a naked woman superimposed on it. Once again, like the concerts that Organisation had played, these were not so much tours of rock clubs, but generally in more esoteric surroundings. Ralf Hütter:

> "We played concerts here and there, at Universities, parties or happenings. We travelled around in a Volkswagen van, living at various friends' houses in other cities. It was not a big organisation like it is today, with stages, container trucks and PA systems."[7]

However, despite these concerts which featured the line-up on the LP, the group was nonetheless to go through a period of turmoil. Hohman was the first to leave and for a short period they continued as a trio. Then, Hütter, Schneider and Dinger were joined by Michael Rother (guitar) and Eberhardt Krahnemann (bass), a five piece line-up which was to only last for one session. Krahnemann's exit was amazingly followed by Hütter himself and for a six month period the group consisted of Schneider, Rother and Dinger. Perhaps not surprisingly the music this trio played bore a closer resemblance to Rother and Dinger's later work with Neu! than it did anything by Kraftwerk.

The trio recorded a 35 minute session at Conny Plank's studio which was never released. However, a good impression of the music they made is a performance that they gave for "The Beatclub" which was filmed and broadcast on German TV in 1971. This first TV performance by Kraftwerk shows Schneider with his flute and electronic equipment, Rother on guitar, and Dinger on drums. They played an eleven minute piece entitled "Truckstop Gondolero" during which they mixed improvised repetitive melodies with the electronic noises provided by Schneider. (This film has recently become available in Japan on video laser-disc, alongside performances by Yes and Soft Machine under the title "Frontiers of Progressive Rock").

Not long after this recording, Rother and Dinger parted company with Schneider and formed Neu!, soon establishing themselves alongside Kraftwerk as the second definitive Düsseldorf cult group. Neu!'s music was a natural extension for Rother and Dinger, taking some of the early Kraftwerk ideas to their logical conclusion. Neu!'s metronomic pulses also drew parallels with Can, and it came as no surprise that Rother would use Can's Jaki Liebezeit as drummer on his later solo recordings.

In any event, when the *Kraftwerk 2* LP was released, Hütter and Schneider had rejoined forces to continue Kraftwerk's electronic ideas. In fact, Rother and Dinger had been involved in early sessions for the LP, but left due to what Rother calmly describes as a "question of temperament, of character".[8] Produced in just seven days between 26th September and 1st October 1971, the LP was recorded at their own studio and the Star Musik Studio in Hamburg. The latter was owned by Ralf Arnie who was a key figure in the Hamburg rock scene and with whom Kraftwerk subsequently signed a publishing deal. The LP is once again co-produced by Conny Plank, whose contribution is acknowledged by a picture credit on the inside sleeve. This may well have been in part a thank you to Plank who believed enough in the music to persuade people like Ralf Arnie to give Kraftwerk cheap and sometimes free access to commercial studios, often working through the night.

Kraftwerk 2, again released on the Philips label, is very much a musical extension of *Kraftwerk*. Certainly the cover concept is a direct continuation, being exactly the same in design, only this time the traffic cone is dayglo green and overprinted with 'Kraftwerk 2'. The idea of making the two covers so similar was probably borrowed from Warhol who would do a series of silkscreens of a particular picture, with only a small colour change between each print. However, copying this trick may have backfired on them. The cover was so similar to the first LP that people might have been forgiven for assuming it was the same record slightly re-packaged.

The double sleeve opens up to reveal mugshots of Hütter and Schneider in various profiles. With leather trousers, long hair, dark glasses and leopard skin jackets, the duo look strangely like members of an early Roxy Music line-up. The bottom row of photos is saved for pictures of the various instruments used on the LP, as if, even then, the instruments (like the studio today) were considered to be additional members of the band.

Kraftwerk 2, like its predecessor, was totally instrumental. Hütter credited with rhythmusmaschine (rhythm machine) as well as a host of other instruments such as the organ, electric piano, glockenspiel, harmonium and bass. Schneider meanwhile is credited with guitar, flute, glockenspiel, and the rather obscure sounding "geige" and "mischpult". The LP found the group developing ways of treating these conventional instruments electronically to create both a new way of playing and a new type of music. Thus piano, flute, guitar and violin are all deformed in an attempt to get away from the sounds normally attributable to them. This way of treating conventional instruments was similar in nature to the music of John Cage amongst others, and in particular his piece called "Prepared Piano".

By this time, having parted company with previous drummers, *Kraftwerk 2* features no conventional drumming at all – the rhythm being produced by a rhythm machine and echo box. At the time, drum machines were very much limited to the sort of rhythm box that could be found in an electric organ and would have a few pre-programmed beats like a bossanova. Ralf Hütter:

> "In 1971 Kraftwerk was still without a drummer, so I bought a cheap drum machine giving some preset dance rhythms. By changing the basic sounds with tape echo and filtering we made the rhythm tracks for our second album. Our instrumental sounds came from home-made oscillators and an old Hammond Organ that gave us various tonal harmonies with its drawbars. We manipulated the tapes at different speeds for further effects."[9]

Because of this reliance on drum machines, the 17 minute "Klingklang" which dominates most of side one has an altogether softer sound than most of the first album, but it is a piece of music that people would recognise as being identifiably Kraftwerk and is undoubtedly the centrepiece of the LP.

The track's constantly shifting tempo is due to the changing beat of the drum machine, giving the impression that for the first time it is a machine that is actually driving the music forward. This in 1971 was a totally new phenomenon. To most people, the very idea that a machine could dictate the form and shape of a piece of music was an alien concept. The track confused the listener further as the tempo almost seems to speed up and slow down at random. Neu! would also use these apparently random tempo changes, only in a more exaggerated way.

"Klingklang", although driven by the rhythm machine, is still characterised by Schneider's breathy flute arpeggios and Hütter's organ playing. Gone is any pretension to improvisation, the whole piece is built with a structure similar to the repetitive patterns in Steve Reich's early music. "Klingklang" stands up today as a remarkable piece, way ahead of its time. The title Klingklang (ring sound in English), was both descriptive of the group's music and a catchy monicker. As such it was not surprising that later records were credited as a Klingklang production, and to this day the two still record in their now-named Kling Klang studio.

Relying more heavily on guitar distortion than drum machine, the second side of *Kraftwerk 2* has an altogether more atmospheric feel. The minimalism of the ideas have an almost child-like simplicity, relying heavily on echo. Being totally uncluttered the tracks often sound as if they are going to peter out altogether like the fading soundtrack to some non-existent film.

So, "Strom" starts with what sounds like breathing or respirator noises, or someone snoring into a microphone. The understated "Wellenlange" is more typical of their later subtlety, but has the added irony of an almost twelve bar blues bass motif coming in toward the end. The LP concludes with "Harmonika" which features Hütter playing repeated arpeggios on the harmonium. The trick of concluding an LP with minimal, arpeggiated phrases, was one which they would use to great effect on later LPs.

On both *Kraftwerk* and *Kraftwerk 2*, Hütter and Schneider were beginning to harness some of the elements that would later lay any comparisons with their improvising compatriots to rest and firmly establish them as the creators of industrial and electronic pop music. However, although these two LPs are often quoted as very important early industrial LPs, they do not conjure up as raw a sound as one would perhaps have expected from the industrial heartland of the Ruhr. Consistent with the care taken over later LPs, the tracks have more of the mechanical touch of light industry without the roaring thunder of heavy machinery.

With the exception of a generally mechanical and Germanic feel, neither of the first two LPs could be described as having any cohesive theme and yet to surface is the group's conceptual approach to the entirety of an LP. Having said that, both LPs have the feeling that their so-called industrial sound is in someways idealised and thus conceptual to a degree. Similar to the altered vision of reality portrayed in the films of Fritz Lang, there was a real hint that there was an ever growing contrast in Kraftwerk between the real world and their idealised vision of it as represented by their music.

Today, although they admit that some of the elements of minimalism on the first two LPs were important precursors to the music they produce now, they are generally non-communicative about them. Florian Schneider:

> "Maybe the idea was to try to achieve a concept, it worked better later, of course. But today we don't consider the first albums as important works, as important compositions. It was another period. Before..."[10]

Hütter, however, denies that they repudiate these early recordings, "No, not at all, it's just that it is an old period so we don't speak so much about it."[11]

Hütter claims that from the very start they made enough money from these early records to be self-sufficient and expand their studio and musical ideas. Although, with both he and Schneider having come from comfortable backgrounds, it is not inconceivable that their musical endeavours were at least in some way subsidised by their respective families. However, initial sales of the first two albums were encouraging, the first LP achieving sales of around 60,000 in Germany. The second LP fared slightly less well, possibly due to their insistence on the confusingly ambiguous cover and title.

Although both LPs were later to become influential recordings, at the time they were still in the shadow of the increasingly popular Can and Tangerine Dream. Can in particular had successfully bridged the gap between experimental and pop music. By the end of 1971 they had a top ten hit in Germany with "Spoon", a track used for the title music of a German TV thriller series, proving that their experimentation could be just as successful within a three minute single format. It would be another three years before Kraftwerk would prove the same point with their own music.

Listening to Kraftwerk's early recordings today, it is probably easier to see in retrospect how detached from the other German groups they actually were at the time. Whilst definitely fitting into the Germanic music scene, they were nonetheless in direct juxtaposition to the traditional instrumentation of Can and Amon Düül in Cologne and Munich respectively, and the Berlin bands who were exclusively infatuated with the new synthesizer. It was noticeable how the German rock scene could be divided into its component parts, the Berlin, Munich and Cologne bands, and the Düsseldorf scene that was centred around Kraftwerk and Neu!

So, whilst the Berlin scene was very "cosmic", the Düsseldorf scene had its own distinctive electronic feel. The groups from Düsseldorf were not interested in goals of musical purity or beauty, but more of creating a new musical language which used every sound source available including industrial technology. As a result, both Kraftwerk and Neu! had a strong physical and rhythmic presence that echoed everyday life.

Because of this, Kraftwerk were beginning to build up a considerable reputation for themselves. Although not yet reflected in world-wide sales, they were also gaining a notoriety further afield for avoiding the norms of rock music that were now being adopted by some of the other German groups. In January 1973, Jean-Pierre Lentin in an edition of the French monthly *Actuel* devoted to the underground in Germany, described Kraftwerk like this:

"Kraftwerk live and play at night. Its musicians are pale, we could think that they are night creatures, vampires maybe. Ralf Hütter wears a black leather suit, white boots, his hair pulled backwards. Phlegmatic and silent, he has lived for the last month in a large empty flat which has not been furnished. It has white walls, a mattress on the floor, and a strange echo in each room.

At midnight he goes out and meets Florian Schneider-Esleben in their studio. They are the founding members of the group, together again after a few adventures. Both have studied classical music but have long since abandoned the old theories. They play flute, violin, guitar, organ – systematically distorting conventional sounds with new ways of playing electronics. Sometimes the music is completely atonal, a pure fascination with noise. To their credit, they have produced two albums which are among the more experimental of German rock, and also among its best sales."[12]

In England too, interest had picked up in German music enough for the first two LPs to appear in 1972 as a double LP on Philips' progressive Vertigo label. The LP appeared in a new sleeve depicting an oscillating blue electronic wave signal which the record company no doubt felt better portrayed the group's electronic music than that of a traffic cone. However, in general it lacked the starkly humorous effect achieved by the original covers.

Subsequently, following their later success, the first two LPs were also re-released in Germany in 1975, as well as selected tracks from *Kraftwerk* and *Kraftwerk 2* being used as the basis of several compilations, but as yet neither LP has been released on Compact Disc, although they have at times expressed an interest in re-releasing these recordings.

It was obvious that Kraftwerk's success was not going to be an overnight affair. The first two LPs had broadly laid out their musical intentions but were too far outside the parameters of rock or pop music to be widely accepted. As such they were more revered by other musicians than by the general public. Even as far back as then, it was clear that Kraftwerk were very much musician's musicians, a situation that despite their world-wide success is still true today. However, if nothing else, the first two LPs had been successful in their attempt to redefine noise and sound as music, and were clearly an influence on a whole myriad of groups who would later include a noise or industrial element to their music.

Ralf Florian

RALF
and
FLORIAN

THE FIRST TWO KRAFTWERK LPS, ALTHOUGH INNOVATIVE IN THEIR own way, had still failed to make any great international impact for the group. By 1972, Can and Tangerine Dream were producing some of their best recorded works and although Kraftwerk were equally creative, they were still considered very much a secondary diversion with a cult following.

There are many reasons why this could have been the case. Certainly, at a time when groups were expected to play live, the public outside of Germany had no performances by which to judge them. In reality, Kraftwerk hadn't been offered that many opportunities. They had taken the decision very early on not to involve themselves in normal rock tours or accept support slots. This was totally different from Can, who had already toured England, or even Tangerine Dream who, despite huge banks of equipment, were also touring regularly. Being essentially perfectionist in outlook, Kraftwerk hadn't yet arrived at the best way of presenting their music live.

Despite this, in February 1973 they accepted an invitation to play their first concert outside of Germany. They took part in a two day festival of German music held at the Théâtre de L'Ouest Parisien in the Boulogne-Billancourt suburb of Paris. The first night featured Kraftwerk and Guru Guru, the second spotlighted Tangerine Dream, Ash Ra Tempel and Klaus Schulze. The festival was organised by the French magazine *Actuel* who had taken a particular interest in some of the new and more interesting bands of the early seventies. Parts of the concerts were also filmed and broadcast by the well-respected French TV music programme *Pop 2*.

The festival was reviewed by Hervé Picart in the French magazine *Best*. In stark contrast to the other groups he described the Kraftwerk set as a "sensational moment". Guru Guru he dismissed as, "a mixture of good and bad, indeed insipid and tasteless." But perhaps his most exacting criticisms were directed at Tangerine Dream:

> "An abstract music, excessively intellectualised, a pure creation of sounds without any search nor any rhythm nor any evocation. A music of a cold empty cosmos, electronic, as distant as these impassible musicians entrenched and immobile behind their desks. Nothing to do with the obsessive poetry of Kraftwerk, which besides is not a spatial group. In short, we are left with the feeling that Tangerine Dream think too much."[1]

Neither Ash Ra Tempel, who he described as having, "a total absence of stage presence", or Klaus Schulze with his "pure abstraction", fared much better.

Picart considered Kraftwerk by far the best of what was on offer as representative of the new German scene. He went on to describe their performance:

> "The group is made up of two contemplative intellectuals, Ralf Hütter (keyboards, electronics) and Florian Schneider-Esleben (flute, violin, keyboards, electronics), coming from Düsseldorf. Their music is very smooth, very slack, a kind of long bewitchment, similar to Terry Riley, made by the prolonging and superimposing of multiple rhythms and circular melodies. The public was surprised at first, by the music alone, then when the lights went off and a screen appeared with luminous arabesques projected onto them, the spell was complete."[2]

Picart's description is typical of early Kraftwerk concerts where the group would appear in total darkness with only the lights from the synchronised back projections as a visual accompaniment. Picart concluded that, "Kraftwerk are an avant-garde group who transform the electronic into the beautiful." Evidently, even this early on, they were conscious of trying to present something that was more of a multi-media event, being visually as well as musically out of the ordinary. In this context, the light show, although not unique to

Kraftwerk, was an early version of the video screens that the group would later use. For Paul Alessandrini, who covered the event for *Actuel* and *Rock & Folk*, it was the first time he had seen the group live:

> "I remember that Ralf still had long hair at this time. On stage their minimalist aspect was already there, Ralf and Florian were alone on stage, each of them had a very small synthesizer. I also remember that between them, from one to the other, there was a sort of transparent plastic tube with lights inside it, it was sort of like an umbilical cord. For me it was all part of a kind of German expressionism, you know, the myth of Doctor Faustus, that sort of thing."[3]

This concert was also the first to utilise their newly built drum machines which they operated themselves. (They may well have been the first ever rock group to use such machines live). They had tried without success to find a drummer willing to operate them, but not surprisingly conventional drummers found the whole concept of being replaced by a machine too radical to consider.

Despite the obvious success of their first concert in Paris, to the rest of the outside world the duo were portraying the same rather studious and anonymous image connected with groups like Tangerine Dream. Picart's obvious enthusiasm aside, excepting the German name and the quirky experimental music, there was still nothing much to set Kraftwerk apart. They were still seen as a curiosity group in Germany, Britain and France, probably exacerbated by the confusing anonymity of the first two LP covers.

The Paris concert highlighted that as the '70s wore on, many of the other German groups' attempts at improvising had begun to lose the plot. The most extreme example was probably Faust whose live concerts were disappointing compared to their records. During some of their live shows they even made a point of ignoring the audience altogether, staring at a television they had brought on stage with them.

What was missing with Kraftwerk was that they had not put as much thought into their image as they had put effort into the music. Hütter and Schneider, being smarter than most, now began to think about acquiring a direct group identity that people could latch onto. It was at this time that Schneider went to see another group who were also making electronic music in Düsseldorf. One of the members of this group was playing a home-made electric violin, something that Schneider at the time was also involved in building, so he invited the musician to come over to Kraftwerk's studio. The violinist turned out to be Emil Schult, who became a close friend of the group, encouraging Hütter and Schneider to adopt the imagery and identity that they had so far lacked.

Schult was born in Düsseldorf, but had spent some time at school in the States. After returning to Germany he became an art student at the Düsseldorf Academy studying under artists Joseph Beuys and Gerhard Richter. His masters degree covered many aspects of the visual media including painting, photography and film, but also brought him into contact with some of the more revolutionary political student movements of the time, including the notorious Daniel Cohn-Bendit, better known as Rote Dany (Red Danny). Bendit was an intellectual who had been a spokesman for the student riots in the Paris "May Revolution" in 1968.

Initially Schult's involvement with Kraftwerk was just a musical one, becoming a regular visitor to their studio, contributing to various jam sessions by playing guitar, flute and the violin that had so intrigued Schneider.

In the early summer of 1973, the group embarked on a German tour, again travelling around the country in a Volkswagen van. They played a set of mostly improvised music, with Hütter on keyboards, Schneider on flute, hawaian guitar and violin, Schult on guitar and electric violin and a friend of Hütter's, Plato Kostic, on bass. (Kostic was also an artist working under the pseudonym Plato Riviera, and today is an architect in Greece). They played various concerts and festivals often to audiences of 2,000 or more, such was the appetite for spontaneous and improvised music at the time. However, it was the basis of this improvisation that would form the backbone to the group's next recording in July 1973.

By the time this LP was released in November of that year, the situation regarding their rather anonymous image was on the way to being rectified. *Ralf And Florian* by its very title put the group on first name familiarity with the record buying public, and to this day is almost synonymous with a nickname for the duo. Adopting their respective first names may well have been influenced by the performance art duo Gilbert and George, who from the late sixties onwards worked exclusively as a single artistic unit under their first names. In any event, the LP's title sustained the minimalist approach of the first two LPs, but was more effective in its simplicity than if they'd merely chosen to continue in the same vein and call it 'Kraftwerk 3'. Both musically, and perhaps more importantly conceptually, they were beginning to hone down their ideas to a few basic concepts and display the clear-sighted approach that would be so prevalent on later LPs.

As well as in their yet-to-be named studio in Düsseldorf, the LP was recorded at the Cornet and Rhenus studios in Cologne and the now defunct but then fashionable Studio 70 in Munich. It was once again co-produced by Conny Plank who helped to organise the recording sessions in the two Cologne studios where he had arrangements with the owners to use them at night.

Due to Schult's influence, the original German cover positively brimmed with humour, as if trying to shrug off the serious experimental image that had surrounded the first two LPs. The front cover features a black and white photo taken by Schneider's then girlfriend Barbara Niemöller, of the duo staring out of the frame with just the hint of a smile on their faces. No longer do they look like musicians but more like eccentric scientists. Interestingly, although Hütter has always been perceived as the leader of the group, it was the now short-haired Schneider who was first to forsake the look of an average rock musician in favour of what was to become the familiar mid-70s Kraftwerk attire of a suit and tie. The addition of a strategically placed minim broach in his jacket lapel also suggested the sophistication of a classical musician.

Schneider's adoption of a formal, almost old-fashioned suit, could again have been inspired by Gilbert and George who chose to juxtapose the newness of their art against an old fashioned image by dressing exclusively in rather stuffy tweed double-breasted suits. Equally likely was that Schneider had abandoned the look of his more rebellious student days, to re-adopt an image more in keeping with his upbringing. Hütter during this period, on the other hand, is still casually dressed and sporting lank long hair and a particularly studious pair of glasses.

For the sake of continuity, the now familiar traffic cone (this time in red and white) with the word Kraftwerk overprinted on it appears in a central position on the front cover between the names Ralf and Florian which are reproduced in a very Germanic typeface.

On the back cover is the most well-known photograph of the inside of the Kling Klang studio. The duo are pictured bathed in a pink and green light. Facing each other, smiling and surrounded by their instruments, they are in exactly the same position as they adopt in the studio today and in the same configuration as when they play live. In front of each of them is a neon sign lit with the words "Ralf" and "Florian" respectively. These signs would become a constant feature of later live performances, not to mention one possible source of inspiration for the track "Neon Lights". Schneider is once again more formally attired, whilst the smoking Hütter sports leather trousers and white Chelsea boots. The familiar traffic cone sits on a speaker at the back of the studio, whilst in the foreground is a rather incongruous looking art-deco lamp from which hangs a plastic pineapple.

The cover, which has the overall appearance of two actors adopting poses like living sculptures, succeeded in injecting some personality and projecting a more humorous image. This tongue-in-cheek approach was further enhanced by what is described as a "comic" included with the initial release of the LP in Germany. The comic was in fact a large opening poster of cartoons and collages describing each track. All the cartoons are humorous and almost childlike, one even features a picture of a bizarre stage set for the group, with weirdly shaped speakers and instruments, which they had at one time actually contemplated building.

Also depicted in sketches or photos are Hütter, Schneider and Schult, as well as a collection of cartoons or photos of what appear to be imaginary women with names like Heidi, Isabella, Tina and Claudia, Eva Maria and Barbara. In reality, Isabella and Barbara were Hütter and Schneider's girfriends at the time, other pictures were of Schneider's sisters and mother, whilst Heidi was the lady from their local record store.

Needless to say, the poster with its cartoon humour was far removed from the sort of thing that was normally associated with serious experimental musicians. The track "Ananas Symphonie" (Pineapple Symphony) for instance is depicted by a guitar plugged into an amplifier in the shape of pineapple. Central to the comic is a futuristic collage which consists of a photo of Düsseldorf coloured in and superimposed with various devices like a walkie-talkie and a set of headphones. Underneath is written in German the sentence, "In Düsseldorf am Rhein klingt es bald" (In Düsseldorf by the Rhine it resonates quickly).

The poster/comic credited as being published by Kling Klang Verlag, was conceived and drawn by Emil Schult with some additional drawings by Schneider, who said that, "When I first met Emil he showed me his comic strips, I found that they looked like our music."[4]

Schult became increasingly instrumental throughout the later '70s in helping to design the group's image and in particular their stage sets. Paradoxically, he was often described as the hidden member of Kraftwerk, being responsible for much of the lighting and visual aspects of the shows, as well as conceiving the record sleeves and writing some of the lyrics. Ralf Hütter once described him as the "medium" of the group. Emil Schult:

> "Yeah, I think that is a good description. Wolfgang (Flur) says I was something like a guru, that I was always there, people would give me their ideas and I would interpret them. I wouldn't say that my talent was especially musical, but you know, I had an influence on everything, that's how it is, when you are in a group you have an influence on everything."[5]

Although having started as a musician within the group, Schult's contribution to *Ralf And Florian* remained solely with the visual image. Hütter and Schneider were adamant that, consistent with the LP's title, they played all the instruments. Certainly, both from the cover photographs and by calling the album *Ralf And Florian*, no-one could really be in any doubt that the group image was now once again back to that of a duo, with Hütter and Schneider credited with all the compositions.

Musically, the LP is a continuation of the ideas on the first two LPs, but in other ways it is also in stark contrast. The general atmosphere of the music is softer and smoother, having a much cleaner sound than either of its predecessors, dominated by electric piano and a softer electronic percussion. Rather than juxtaposing the mechanical sounds against a backdrop of the music, now they were being incorporated into the music itself.

"Elecktrisches Roulette" ("Electric Roulette") which opens side one is a rhythmically repetitive piece, bearing as close a resemblance to the later Kraftwerk sound as anything from the first two self-titled LPs. The track features electronics, electric piano, violin and drums, and despite its free-form moments has the first signs of discernably constructed pop melodies. This is followed by "Tongebirge" ("A Mountain Range Of Tones") which is more like earlier LPs and sees Schneider's typical flute arpeggios treated to a heavy dose of echo.

"Kristallo" followed their practice of looking close to home for inspiration being the name of a hotel near to their studio. It features clear repetitive keyboard arpeggios showing Hütter further developing the automaton feel to his playing, starting off patterns that almost seem to continue on their own. The track ends like a catalogue of various recording tricks including backwards tapes, and a speeded up section that sounds a little like The Chipmunks play the classics.

"Heimatklange" ("The Sounds Of Homeland") which closes side one demonstrates the duo's increasing grasp of dynamics by following the technical trickery of "Kristallo" with a simple almost chamber music melody for piano and flute.

Side two opens with "Tanzmuzik" ("Dance Music") which is Hütter and Schneider's first conscious effort to produce a kind of dance music, albeit a rather strange hybrid variety. Dance music and dancing were to become an obsession for the group later on, but here the dance beat is only a very minimal backbone to the piece. Throughout the track very simple wooden and metallic noises provide a fascinating extra percussive feel to the ever present rhythm box. Towards the end, actual hand claps appear, as if bridging the gap between the avant-garde nature of Steve Reich's "Clapping Music" and the dance music of Motown. However, perhaps the most notable break from tradition is the inclusion of a vocal, albeit with no words, indicating their first tentative step away from being a totally instrumental group.

The final track "Ananas Symphonie" is the customary longer workout featuring some slide guitar which gives the track its strangely Hawaian feel – the tropical theme of the music presumably prompting the quirky title. The track has a moody laziness and meanders in a rather minimal way, relying more on a hypnotic element rather than the dynamics used on some of the longer tracks on previous LPs. Most important is the emergence of a primitive vocoder through which the words 'Ananas Symphonie' are clearly discernable. The existence of an electronic way of treating voices had obviously given the duo the confidence to think about using a vocal lyric for the first time, albeit very understated. As with the introduction of the drum machine, once again a development in their music had been dictated by a technical innovation, showing an ever-increasing fascination with electronic sound effects.

By projecting a real group image, Kraftwerk were now running ahead of fellow Düsseldorf group Neu! who by 1973 had recorded two LPs under the guiding hand of Conny Plank. Following in Kraftwerk's footsteps, Neu!'s records were entitled *Neu!* and *Neu! 2*. Similarly their LP covers echoed earlier Kraftwerk records by being very simple in design and featuring small passport sized photos of the group. (Incidentally, by 1975 Neu! had run out of steam, having produced a final LP appropriately called *Neu! '75*, featuring Rother, Dinger and two extra drummers. Michael Rother then went on to make a series of solo LPs, whilst Klaus Dinger went on to form another Düsseldorf cult group called La Düsseldorf, lasting a number of years and producing three LPs.)

Even though *Ralf And Florian* displayed many of the familiar and distinctive Kraftwerk musical trademarks, it is still the kind of LP which is associated with a cult group. It is true that their ideas had now been boiled down to a more recognisable shape with the inclusion of some vocals and sequenced keyboards, but somehow the LP is still not a conclusive whole despite being more image conscious. The feeling of the music is still of a film soundtrack variety, with only a slight inclination toward a pop music mentality or lyrical structure.

Later, when *Ralf And Florian* was released in the UK, it appeared in a far less interesting cover depicting an electrical circuit. This totally denied the type of "Ruhr Brothers" irony that accompanied the original sleeve with its obvious humorous connection with the title. Overall, like its predecessors, the LP sold moderately well at the time. However, following the success that awaited the group just around the corner, the LP did slightly better. When reissued in October 1975 it even reached No 160 in the US charts. Like the group's first two LPs, *Ralf and Florian* has yet to surface on Compact Disc.

AUTOMOBILES
and
MOTORWAYS

QUITE WHAT HAPPENED IN THE MINDS OF HÜTTER AND SCHNEIDER between the release of *Ralf And Florian* in November 1973 and its successor in November of the following year, can only be a matter of conjecture. Although many of the elements of the Kraftwerk sound are recognisable in their first three LPs, it doesn't really account for the quantum leap in their development that the *Autobahn* LP represented. In the space of a year Hütter and Schneider had mostly dropped any notions of continuing with the avant-garde nature of their first three LPs. More importantly, with the continuing help of Emil Schult, they had begun perfecting a highly stylised Germanic image, a total rounded package that was now identifiably unique to Kraftwerk. As Lester Bangs put it, "More than just a record, it is an *indictment*."[1]

By the beginning of 1974, it was becoming obvious to the duo that success was more likely to come from the regimentation afforded by the latest technology, rather than the hit or miss process of improvisation. As a result, Hütter and Schneider took the decision to follow some of their German contemporaries and invest in a mini-Moog synthesizer. This decision was made easier by the group's financial independence, allowing them to buy what was then very expensive equipment – Hütter now remembers it being as expensive as a Volkswagen, the price of which has always been a German economic barometer. Not long after its purchase, Hütter and Schneider realised that the synthesizer was perfect for their increasingly disciplined music, and that their musical development was now building toward an inevitable electronic future. Soon, they were harbouring designs that this new technology could become the star and they were just the catalysts that brought it all together.

For this reason *Autobahn*'s success must be partially put down to the adoption of the technology that allowed drum machines to be linked to synthesizers via sequencers. This meant that the long repetitive pieces in their music, which had previously been made haphazard by human innacuracy or lack of stamina, could now be replaced by machines that would faultlessly reproduce repetitive patterns ad infinitum. It is quite surprising to think that compared with groups like Tangerine Dream, Kraftwerk were actually quite late to pick up on the synthesizer. Up until that point they had actually been rather conservative, preferring to treat conventional instruments electronically. However, having decided to join the synthesizer race, they lost no time in applying their own particular uniqueness to the instrument.

Out of all the German groups who were fascinated with the synthesizer, only Kraftwerk were adventurous enough to investigate its pop potential. Tangerine Dream and all their cohorts had quickly jumped on its application as a new sound source, but had all too readily become lost in a sort of quasi-classical netherworld. This was compounded by musicians such as Walter Carlos (now Wendy Carlos following a sex change) and Tomita whose first reaction when presented with a new method of creating sound, was to replace the orchestra and recreate the classics. Likewise, both Brian Eno and Keith Emerson, although at different ends of the musical spectrum, were incorporating it as an instrument within a more traditional rock band format. Hütter and Schneider's more up front "poppier" approach enabled them to leapfrog much of the competition and produce one of the first synthesizer pop records.

However, in terms of purely pop music, it was not completely the first. An interesting diversion had been caused a couple years previously by Hot Butter's 1972 instrumental single "Pop Corn". At the time this was dismissed as a novelty or gimmick record. But with its totally synthesized tune created by an anonymous looking group, it now appears way ahead of its time. As it was a one-off record, nobody in the music business yet believed that synthesizers and drum machines could provide a credible alternative to guitars and drums.

Today, synthesizers and sampling equipment are everyday norms in the recording process. It is easy to overlook how revolutionary it was to attempt to create a totally synthesized pop music. In the early '70s, attitudes towards machines replacing conventional instruments were very reactionary. It was generally thought that it was a cheat perpetrated by people who couldn't play proper instruments, or a plot to deprive regular musicians from earning a living. One commentator even went as far as to suggest that Kraftwerk were the death of music. In reality, most people were missing the point. Far from being the death of anything, it was more like the birth of a new type of music. Kraftwerk almost single-handedly went on to prove that electronic music *had* to be taken seriously, brushing aside any criticism as backward looking and unchallenging.

The result of Kraftwerk's startlingly quick mastery of the complexities of the Moog was the *Autobahn* album, recorded at their recently christened Kling Klang studio and at Conny Plank's new studio. After spending most of the early '70s working in Cologne and Hamburg, Plank had finally established his own studio in 1973 in a converted farmhouse outside Cologne – the studio room being the old pigsty and the control booth converted from the stables. It was on Plank's mobile equipment that much of *Autobahn* was conceived.

As if to herald a new era for the group, the LP cover was more complex, and conspicuous by its absence was the traditional trademark of the traffic cone. Instead, the front cover is a painting by Emil Schult which juxtaposes images of the countryside, mountains, an exaggerated sun, green grass, blue sky and floating clouds, against the most potent symbol of the industrial era – the motor car on the motorway. The cover also juxtaposes two symbols of the world-wide economic success of post-war Germany. On the left a big black Mercedes symbolises a rich upper class form of transport, whilst the white Volkswagen Beetle on the right typifies a mode of transport for the middle and working classes. The painting also has an idealised, dream-like quality as there are no other cars to be seen, as if depicting an ideal world where there is little or no traffic and no pollution.

Autobahn's imagery is rooted in a particular time when Germans were taking full advantage of the road building programme that had been undertaken during and after the second World War. Most German families now owned a car and could drive around the countryside at ever increasing speeds. In some ways, the idea of the family car and the motorway were a continuation of Hitler's vision of a Volkswagen (or people's car) coupled with good transport links.

However, rather than portraying reality, Kraftwerk's particular autobahn was an idealised notion of the motorway – as conjured up from within the walls of the Kling Klang studio. This represented a hypothetical, and somewhat romanticized image of road transport, but nonetheless an artistically appealing one. Florian Schneider:

> "We have recently been in ex-East Germany and the highways are really still like that, except there is a lot more traffic. But even for us, *Autobahn* is a bit nostalgic now, even in the '70s our image of the autobahn was a bit idealised."[2]

The idea for the LP's title track was apparently born out of a drive the group had taken in Hütter's Volkswagen, a tape recorder hanging out of the window recording the sounds of the traffic. Schult now remembers the concept being born in the studio, inspired by the noises coming from their newly aquired Moog. Either way, from the very opening noise of a car starting up, the whole piece can be conceived as a car journey. With the use of stereo, passing car noises and hooting horns swept across the speakers. But the real surprise was the inclusion of words or phrases, signifying that for the first time Kraftwerk had constructed a sort of song. Emil Schult:

> "We just came up with this concept; 'let's do a song like driving on the autobahn'. Ralf specifically asked me to write some lyrics, and I wrote them, in fact it took me one day, I brought them back, Ralf went over them and corrected them a little bit, and it was singable, so it became a song."[3]

In the group's eyes the track was much more than just a song or a piece of music. It was clear that they had started to apply some of the strictly regimented conceptual criteria that they were later to apply so dogmatically to each piece of music. Hütter was now clearly enjoying this conceptual side that allowed him to theorise, often humourously, about its derivation:

"You can listen to "Autobahn" and then go and drive on the motorway. Then you will discover that your car is a musical instrument. In these sorts of ideas, there are plenty of things that can be funny; it's a whole philosophy of life which comes from electronics."[4]

For recording the LP, Hütter and Schneider were accompanied by additional musicians Klaus Roeder (violin and guitar) and Wolfgang Flur (percussion). On the back cover, the four are seen sitting in the back of a car, behind them the motorway stretches into the distance. In fact, the original picture was actually of Hütter, Schneider, Roeder and Schult, but on the final sleeve Flur's head has been grafted onto Schult's body, giving the picture the appearance of a collage. Schult himself appears as a small circular photo on the dashboard.

Both Flur and Roeder had been hired from the small Düsseldorf music scene, where everyone involved in music tended to know each other. Flur, born in Frankfurt am Main on 17th July 1947, was an interior design student who had drummed for a while in a local Düsseldorf band called The Beethovens – Michael Rother played guitar for some time in the same band whose repertoire consisted mainly of chart music. Flur, together with Roeder's later replacement Karl Bartos, would remain Hütter and Schneider's longest standing musical collaborators over subsequent years.

Hütter and Schneider, in direct contrast to their current isolation, were actually an integral part of this Düsseldorf music scene. In fact, during the early '70s various members of Kraftwerk shared a large flat in the centre of town. Hütter, Schult and Flur all stayed here from time to time. Looking back, Bartos now describes the flat as a kind of "open house with plenty of parties".[5] However, possibly due to the numbers of people hanging around, the more solitary Hütter's stay was a short one, having already left by the time Bartos moved in.

On the LP sleeve Hütter and Schneider themselves are merely credited with vocals and electronics, in a visible attempt to get away from the idea of being perceived as conventional musicians. Nor, despite its use, is there the slightest mention of the word synthesizer, probably as it had become too closely associated with the cosmic German rock bands as their stalwart instrument. Hütter and Schneider almost seemed to be implying that they were now way beyond both traditional instruments and their musical counterparts. One play of *Autobahn* and it was evident that this seemingly arrogant assumption was right.

Such was their confidence in the track "Autobahn", that for the first time they took the more conventional step of titling the LP after the track. Although all the previous LPs had featured long tracks, for the first time since the Organisation LP, a single track took up the whole of one side. By adopting a 'concept' it gave the album an identity, enabling people, and particularly critics, to view it in more of a rock music context – after all it was not uncommon in 1974 for such diverse groups as Jethro Tull, The Grateful Dead and Yes to take up a whole side, or even sometimes two, with one track.

This once again could have put Kraftwerk back in a category with the 'conceptual rock' of Pink Floyd or King Crimson. But what made *Autobahn*'s title track unique, was that it was not a classical rock symphony with parts and movements, it was in effect one very long pop song, even if only minimally based around a traditional verse and chorus. This, coupled with the startlingly modern sheen to the music, meant that they were finally able to brush any such comparisons aside as superficial and irrelevant. Suddenly, Kraftwerk had dusted themselves down and discarded most of their remaining hippyish trappings (although from the picture on the sleeve Schneider was still alone in having visited a hairdresser in the recent past). Nevertheless, they seemed poised to emerge as leaders of an electronic music that was as modern in image as the synthesizer was in technology.

Initially, reaction to the LP in Germany was guarded. The group invited various members of the German rock press to drive around with them, the track blaring from the speakers in the car. Schult remembers that the general response from the journalists was an emphatic, "So what!". Conceptually, it was perhaps all a bit too close to home for them to appreciate. It was only when the track came to be recognised in the USA and the rest of Europe as a specifically Germanic statement that the German press paid them more attention. Not for the last time the group began to sense a certain hostility in their home country to their conceptualising of a German lifestyle. Many artists were actually quite critical of Kraftwerk. Klaus Schulze, for example, said, "Kraftwerk are theories, only theories." Others were wary that they were just poking fun at all things German. Emil Schult:

"I think what happened with "Autobahn" was that the importance in a cultural sense was more appreciated by foreigners than by Germans. It is strange that people from America, France or England realised more what it meant than people in Germany did. I personally was a bit disappointed that these cultural achievements were not credited very much in our home country. The commercial success seemed more important to people than the cultural significance."[6]

Paul Alessandrini:

"They have always made use of stereotypes, it's like they say, "We came from a country which evokes a certain type of imagery, a lot of clichés, so let's play this game, let's transform ourselves into these stereotypes."[7]

Despite scepticism at home, the track quickly acquired a certain anthemic quality, soon turning into a kind of "Route 66" for the seventies. Rock music has always had a fascination with driving, but whilst "Route 66" represented images of drifting across America in the 60's, "Autobahn" reflected the connection between the concrete monotony of the highway and daily life. Also, by choosing such an apparently everyday theme, they may well have been trying to break away from the 'Kraut Rock' tradition of dealing with quasi "cosmic" themes. However, their initial attempts to do so were not totally successful. For instance, a concert at the Bataclan in Paris on March 12th, 1975 was advertised with the slogan "musik cosmik".

Autobahn, released in November 1974, was somewhat of a shock for Kraftwerk fans who had invested both time and money becoming acquainted with the first three less commercial LPs. Suddenly, the haphazard, improvised feel had been replaced by a snappy regimented tune and something that approximated a conventional pop lyric. Like many of their subsequent pieces, it is really less of a lyric and more of a minimal vocal accompaniment which, rather than telling a story, merely punctuates the music. Obviously the words add meaning, but there is also a sense of them being used purely for their phonetic sound, almost like a nursery rhyme, with the famous line, "wir fahr'n fahr'n fahr'n auf der autobahn". The words as they are sung almost sound English, "fun, fun, fun on the autobahn" sounding reminiscent of The Beach Boys. It is typical of the detached and mechanically half-spoken way that they would later use phrases in German, English and French alike, merely for the sound of them, without purposefully working in one language or another. As Hütter explained to Geoff Barton in *Sounds*:

> "We use language also as a musical instrument. It's like when we sing. People say it's too low, we cannot understand the singer. But we are not singers in the sense of Rod Stewart, we use our voices as another instrument. Language is just another pattern of rhythm, it is one part of our unified sound."[8]

However, as well as being rhythmical, the vocoded and harmonised vocal to "Autobahn" shows the clear influence of The Beach Boys. Although, "We are not aiming so much for the music; it's the psychological structure of someone like The Beach Boys."[9], they explained to Lester Bangs. Some people still use the nickname of "The Beach Boys from Düsseldorf", which apparently originated in the American music press following the release of the "Autobahn" single. The fact that this nickname emanated from a journalist coming from The Beach Boys' home country added irony, rather than if it had been dreamt up by a European journalist. To some, the real comparison between the two groups might seem quite slight, but The Beach Boys' notorious studio marathons and approach to perfection had, and still has, certain similarities with the way Kraftwerk operate.

Whilst Kraftwerk were no doubt flattered at the time to be compared with their idols, by 1991, when asked whether he liked the nickname, Schneider offered a cagey response:

> "No, not so much... The Beach Boys belong to their own category. You know, describing the image of Kraftwerk is not my job! (laughs) It's always very difficult to say something about yourself."[10]

The title track is so dominating, it would be easy to give the impression that the whole *Autobahn* LP was a complete break with their past. However, it can be split into two distinct halves. Whilst the "Autobahn" side concentrates on the hypnotic elements of the long title track, the second side brings together some of the more melodic elements of earlier LPs.

Side two opens with "Kometenmelodie 1" and "Kometenmelodie 2" ("Comet Melody 1 & 2"). Despite its rather cosmic title, the two-part piece shows how the group were beginning to explore what could be done with a very simple melody. "Kometenmelodie 1" is very slow whilst in "Kometenmelodie 2" the tempo speeds up to find its natural rhythm. It is in some ways a throwback to the *Ralf and Florian* LP, playing around with almost danceable ideas. Most groups would have probably settled for only presenting the finished version of such a piece, i.e. "Kometenmelodie 2", but they chose also to include "Kometenmelodie 1" which sounds like a slow 'demo' of the track as if they wanted to show how the melody had come about. The result, although not very listenable, is interesting for that in itself.

"Mitternacht" ("Midnight") is a short piece that could have been written as the soundtrack to a short horror movie. Ironically, the first minute of the track could have been lifted from a Tangerine Dream LP of the same period. Possibly Kraftwerk were poking fun at those types of groups by saying, "look, you do it for five hours, but we know how to do it in one minute!" However, the electronic sound and the way the track develops, bears much closer comparison with the musique concrete of Pierre Henry.

"Morgenspaziergang" ("Morning Walk") is another of their scraps of melody reminiscent of previous LPs. Schneider's flute (or possibly synthesized flute) is accompanied by small electronic and synthetic noises. Despite its throwaway aspect, it is a good example of the way that Kraftwerk were beginning to effectively harness the atmospheres that they were trying to recreate in the studio – in this case a morning walk. It has a cartoon-like simplicity, like a Walt Disney soundtrack for the animated recreation of the dawning of a new day.

Autobahn's impact was not long in coming. By the beginning of 1975, an edited single version of the title track was receiving a rather surprising amount of airplay in the USA where a radio station in Chicago had picked up on the single as an import. As a result, Jem Records in New Jersey were soon importing considerable quantities of the LP. Capitol were quick to seize on its potential and released both the single and the LP in the States. At first glance the decision to hack a 22 minute atmospheric track to the length of a single might have appeared like a potentially unsuccessful ploy by their record company. But strangely enough, when edited down to four minutes it took on a life of its own, approximating a very conventional song, making the most of its verse/chorus/verse structure. As a result the "Autobahn" single was soon receiving massive airplay on both the FM progressive stations and the AM mainstream stations, becoming the first record with German lyrics to enter the US charts – reaching No 25. It was even reported to be a particular favourite of certain chapters of Hell's Angels. It also charted at No 11 in the UK in the same month, staying on the chart for 11 weeks. Subsequently, on the strength of the single, the LP went on to reach No 4 in the UK charts and peaked at No 5 in the US where it stayed on the chart for 22 weeks. (Americans were perhaps more receptive to *Autobahn* than expected as the trail had in part been blazed for them by the success of Pink Floyd's *Dark Side of the Moon* and Mike Oldfield's *Tubular Bells* the previous year.)

It was as if Hütter and Schneider had suddenly hit the jackpot. From being perceived as two rather serious-minded experimental musicians with a limited following, they now had a hit single on both sides of the Atlantic on their hands. At the time, the group no doubt claimed that this step was just a natural extension of their previous work, but on the face of it, it was difficult not to assume that certain very positive commercial decisions had been made at the Kling Klang studio. Just as the autobahn was the fastest most direct route from one place to another, so Kraftwerk had made an equally speedy transition into the limelight. Even previously, the group had not been totally unaware of their commercial potential – one of the factors that had attracted Kraftwerk to the Phonogram group in the first place was their ability to promote singles on both sides of the Atlantic.

So, whilst Can and Tangerine Dream were still nibbling away at the fringes of rock respectability, Kraftwerk had suddenly been catapulted into stardom. Almost in one deft turn of the musical dial, they had now leapfrogged the rest of German rock music, making Amon Düül II, Tangerine Dream and many others look old hat.

1975 couldn't have been a better year for Kraftwerk to make their initial impact on a mass market. Not many groups were making interesting or challenging records, and people were getting tired of the complacency and cliches of pompous rock bands like Yes and Jethro Tull – whilst Punk was a revolution still waiting to happen. Also, European music was beginning to be treated as less of a joke. The sudden and meteoric rise to fame of Abba showed that a pop band could achieve world-wide status without being British or American – despite the burden of having won the *Eurovision Song Contest*! All this conspired to make the *Autobahn* LP a perfect statement of its time, released in a vacuum of its own making, but a record that it would take a lot of bands another few years to catch up with. *Autobahn* placed Kraftwerk at the forefront of European music, influencing a host of other European groups over the next decades. Patrick Codenys of Front 242:

> "In the early '70s the majority of the, let's say creative groups, were virtuosos like King Crimson and Yes whose music was based around sophisticated jam sessions. When I bought *Autobahn* I had the feeling that it was changing. For the first time it was music that was impossible to touch – not being made up with the usual components of rock. I had the feeling that it was all done by only one person. This helped me to think, "Why can't I make music on my own?"
>
> At that time, Krafwerk represented the natural following step after Can, Tangerine Dream and Neu! by bringing something more precise. They were the first group to express a discipline, a process."[11]

It is interesting that Patrick Codenys states that when he first heard *Autobahn* he had the feeling that it was all done by one person. Then as now, the group are reticent to talk about who does what, but by *Autobahn* quite possibly most of the music was being written by Hütter, and embellished by Schneider. (This may well still be the case. In 1991, when asked what exactly his role in Kraftwerk was, Schneider replied laughing, "I don't know, you must ask Ralf."[12])

In the Spring of 1975, Kraftwerk took another uncharacteristically commercial decision and toured abroad to maximise the success of *Autobahn*. To do the new material justice, Hütter and Schneider realised it would be pointless touring as a duo. For a short tour of Germany at the end of 1974, they remained a foursome by retaining percussionist Wolfgang Flur, and hiring another electronic percussionist Karl Bartos in favour of Klaus Roeder. The aim was to give the new material a crisper more percussive edge. Also, by replacing Roeder (who went on to pursue a solo project), Hütter and Schneider had mostly rid the group of the last vestiges of conventional instruments – in essence the guitar and violin were now redundant (interestingly Schneider's flute survived for a while longer).

It was also unlikely that Roeder with his waist length hair and beard would ever have fitted into the group's new image. In fact, very soon after the LP's release, Hütter decided that they should follow Schneider's example and adopt a more disciplined and coherent approach to their appearance. Out went the long hair and casual clothes and in came suits, ties and shorter hair styles. Now that the music was more regimented, so the group themselves adhered to a more business-like look that was less like that of a normal rock group and more like that of company executives.

By presenting Kraftwerk as a foursome, it gave their group image a more complete roundness. Indeed, it would have been very difficult to sustain the corporate image that they were now outwardly portraying with just two people. With the four of them, they were far more synonymous with a traditional pop group line-up, rather than the sort of electronic Gilbert and George image they had achieved as musicians within the avant-garde scene. The impression of a foursome was somewhat of an illusion, as Bartos and Flur were hired musicians. Hütter and Schneider continued to do all the interviews and write all of the material. The main driving force would remain Ralf and Florian as their previous LP title had stressed so strongly.

Whilst Wolfgang Flur had come from the local rock scene, Karl Bartos was a 22 year old music student at the Robert Schumann Conservatorium in Düsseldorf. Bartos, born in Berchtesgarden on 31st May 1952, was studying at the Conservatorium with the hope of obtaining a regular job as a percussionist with the Berlin Symphony Orchestra. Hütter knew Bartos' professor at the Conservatorium and called saying that they needed a classically trained percussionist for their upcoming touring schedule. Bartos recalls his first meeting with the group being when he ran into Hütter, Schneider and Schult playing pool at the Institute. It wasn't long before he was being picked up in Hütter's VW van for a rehearsal at the Kling Klang studio.

Initially, both Bartos and Flur had been hired to do a very specific job as percussionists. Clearly, Hütter and Schneider had a very distinct idea of the mechanical type of percussion that they now wanted to accompany their music. Bartos admits that he found this initial restriction boring at times, "like there were no offbeats, and if I played offbeats they were rather disturbed by it."[13] Being a classically trained musician it was conceivable that Bartos found being suddenly immersed in the Kraftwerk set up somewhat strange. Karl Bartos:

"At that time it was just a job for me. I had days when I would rehearse at the Opera House in the morning, at noon I was giving lessons to students and in the afternoon I would play at the Kunstakademie, and in the evening I would play Lohengrin. And after that came Kraftwerk.

As a student I had already played percussion at various concerts in Germany – works by Karlheinz Stockhausen, Mauricio Kagel, things like that. I was very used to electronic music. I remember thinking that with the four of us, Kraftwerk looked a bit like an odd string quartet. Concerning the clothes, it was basically the same, I had to wear a suit to perform classical contemporary things, I also had to wear a suit with Kraftwerk!"[14]

So, in April 1975, following a couple of dates in Europe, Hütter, Schneider, Flur and Bartos set off for their first trip to America. The 22-date tour had been organised by Ira Blacker, a former rock promoter, who had been enterprising enough to get Kraftwerk and a number of other German bands to sign up for management deals in the States. A couple of weeks into the tour they were joined by Schult, who was more familiar with the country, having lived in the States for a year when he was eighteen. The strange paradox of four German guys bringing a new form of electronic rock music to the home of rock 'n' roll was not lost on the group. As Ralf Hütter recalls, "Late at night, we stopped at a café along the road in a remote part of Florida, and from the jukebox "Autobahn" was escaping."[15]

With a single riding high in the American charts the tour was obviously going to be a fairly prestigious affair and included an appearance on the *Midnight Special* TV programme. The starkly presented live shows with minimal equipment and neon lights were in direct opposition to the kind of shows that Tangerine Dream were putting on. The set featured almost the whole of their *Autobahn* LP, together with some of their earlier material, but despite a top five album, the concerts were not universally well received. At one performance in Berkeley, California, Todd Tolces for the *Melody Maker* estimated the audience to be about 150 people. He went on to describe a concert where "the band's overall vibrations fell just short of intolerable eeriness". Clearly Tolces was shocked at a group who paid so little regard to the audience, and where the set seemed to rely on automation. Perhaps not surprisingly he was one of many who thought that this was a gimmick which would be short lived:

> "It's beyond me how their album broke into the US charts but here it is defying all trends and previous speculations. It reminds me of the freak incidents like the T-Bones "No Matter What Shape (Your Stomach's In)" from the Alka Seltzer commercials, and "I'd Like To Buy The World A Coke" which was rearranged to blast, "I'd Like To Teach The World To Sing" from the New Seekers.
>
> See, freaks *do* come from all over the world... not just Madison Avenue advertising agencies."[16]

Exactly what was on tape and what was played live, then as now, provided fans and critics alike with a talking point. However, a good idea of what was presented to American audiences that year is given by a short concert the group recorded in the confines of the studios at Cologne Radio FM. This shows how marked the differences between the recorded LP and live performances were in those days. The concert begins with a powerful 9 minute rendition of "Ruckzuck" off the first *Kraftwerk* LP. The piece is reworked with the two new electronic drummers providing the percussion. Hütter plays piano and electronics accompanied by Schneider on flute and electronics, his flute playing sounding a bit like an exaggerated Ian Anderson.

The rest of the performance is taken up with pieces from *Autobahn*. In stark contrast to the first piece which is played very professionally, both "Kometenmelodie 1 & 2" and a 25 minute version of "Autobahn" sound weak in comparison. The tempo of both pieces is much slower than on the LP and the music seems to hiccup and falter as if they hadn't yet fully come to terms with the potential of their equipment.

Audiences who may have only been acquainted with the recorded versions must have been confused by the live renditions.

Part of the problem was that the early synthesizers were notoriously unreliable and difficult to tune. Often they had to be turned on in the afternoon in order to be in tune for the evening. Even then, the heat from the audience or the lighting rig would easily put them out of tune again. These problems were further exacerbated by the differences in voltage between different countries. At the time, Germany worked on 220 volts at 50 hertz whilst France operated on 110 volts at 60 hertz. Ralf Hütter:

> "I remember well that we played in Paris on 110 volts and all the tempos were out of tune. At 8 p.m. the big factories that plug into the network were making the voltage fluctuate. That's the reality, Peugeot were making our tempos change. The engineer that was travelling with us had to install stabilizers."[17]

With a major hit single and a tour underway, it was obvious that they were going to receive their first real exposure to media attention. The duo's response to this was probably the biggest masterstroke of their career, and one to which they have remained unnervingly faithful. This was to create a persona or aura around the band in the way that they chose to answer questions. Hütter and Schneider intrigued interviewers with talk of the sensitivity of machines and how they reacted when they were played; "Sometimes we play the music, sometimes the music plays us, sometimes... it plays"[18], Hütter informed the UK rock weekly *Sounds* following the group's concert at the Hammersmith Odeon in November 1975. Rather than making excuses, they exaggerated the very aspect of automation within their music that could very well have been the biggest criticism of the band. They even began to talk of an ideal situation where the machines toured by themselves.

Of course, the critics and public loved it. Here was a totally new way of presenting a rock band. Not the overtly fun-loving, drug-taking, girl chasing, long-haired stereotypes that journalists had become accustomed to, but serious theoreticians with short hair and suits who espoused and praised all things German. For the first time ideas like

Menschmachine (Man-machine) started to crop up in their conversations. Karl Bartos:

"The initial image really came from Ralf. He wanted to make it clear that Kraftwerk were different from any other pop or rock group and he wanted this image of a string ensemble. I didn't like it that much, I thought I always looked like a banker. I liked it better when we changed to the black shirt and trousers."[19]

For their pains, the critics responded in turn by enhancing the group's theories with descriptions of the music, like "industrial folk music" ("Industrielle Volkmuzik"). Hütter and Schneider were happy to embrace these new tags, perhaps as a way of further isolating them from any 'Kraut Rock' or rock music comparisons. Although agreeing to interviews, and happy to talk of their technological obsessions, Hütter and Schneider now closed down on any talk of themselves as individuals. They adopted the deliberate ploy of sublimating themselves as musicians in favour of the group's corporate image, refusing to be drawn on the human elements of their lives, in favour of robotic one liners. They were equally as shy concerning publicity photographs. In one of the group's most illuminating interviews with the late Lester Bangs of *Creem* Magazine, when asked to pose for a photo, they refused, and when asked why – they replied, "because we are paranoid."[20]

In 1975, they were less practised in their particular art of non-communication or "robotspeak", and Bangs managed to occasionally get behind their steely wall of mystique. He persuaded Hütter and Schneider to drop their guard long enough to admit a liking for the MC5 and Lou Reed, and the conclusion that they found the Blue Oyster Cult funny! Incrongruous as it might seem now, Hütter and Schneider were rather taken with the American thrash guitar bands of the early seventies. Despite later claims of not being musicians, they were knowledgeable about a wide range of music as Marc Zermati, founder of the legendary French label Skydog, remembers:

"Once when Ralf Hütter and Florian Schneider were in Paris around 1976, they visited the shop I had in Les Halles called the Open Market. I was very surprised because I was not really into their kind of music, I was more into rock 'n' roll. We all went back to my home and they began to look at my record collection. They picked out records by the MC5, Iggy and the Stooges, and they were very interested in the sound of these records, particularly the way the guitars were saturated. They not only had a perfect knowledge of rock but also jazz like Mingus and Coltrane. Later, I became interested myself in their music, and despite the fact that it is not really the sort of thing I prefer, I realised that Kraftwerk definitely occupy a strong place in the history of music."[21]

Autobahn, which was recorded for next to nothing compared with other LPs of the time, went on to become a top selling LP. Somewhat fortuitously for the group, it was the last of a three album deal that they had with Philips, which meant that they could look around for a new contract armed with a top ten LP on both sides of the Atlantic. The result was a world-wide licensing deal for their newly established Kling Klang company with EMI. This meant Electrola for Germany, Austria and Switzerland (or GAS as it's known), EMI in the UK, Capitol in America, and Pathé-Marconi in France.

Following on from the success of the "Autobahn" single, Philips released a second single. "Kometenmelodie 2", however, lacked the attractive simplicity of the truncated version of "Autobahn" and failed to chart. This fuelled speculation amongst the more cynical elements in the music press, who pondered whether in terms of singles the group might perhaps be classed as one-hit wonders.

Inevitably, for an LP which was to be regarded as a classic watershed album in the history of pop music, when Compact Discs became available, it wasn't long before a digitally re-mixed version appeared simultaneously on CD, LP and cassette in 1985. On the CD version Conny Plank's name has been taken off the sleeve. An unfortunate oversight or strange decision considering the input he had made to the early Kraftwerk sound? Either way it was something about which Plank himself was apparently astonished, especially as he was convinced of the imaginative input he had contributed to the musical philosophy of the group.

In fact, *Autobahn* was to be the last Kraftwerk LP that Conny Plank would engineer, and after its success he had the feeling that he had been dropped, somehow kicked off the project. From that point on there was no contact between the group and their former engineer. In strict terms, the severing of ties was probably inevitable. In reality, Plank had probably outlived his usefulness, as they strove for ever greater self-sufficency. Despite being left out of further recordings, Plank's reputation was undoubtedly connected with Kraftwerk, and this was probably one of the main reasons why he was approached by other groups to do production work.

Plank himself continued working in his studio which came to be known as "Conny's Studio". Here he produced many acts like Killing Joke, Eno, Eurythmics and Devo, as well as European groups and artists like La Düsseldorf, Neu!, Michael Rother, DAF, Gianna Mannini, Les Rita Mitsouko and Clannad. He also worked with Holger Czukay on his groundbreaking *Movies* LP, but his most famous production remains Ultravox's "Vienna" which became an international hit. However, despite his success he refused offers to expand the studio, wishing to keep its almost private and intimate atmosphere. The studio still exists today and is run by Plank's widow Krista Fast.

Plank died in December 1987, having worked with most of the major German bands. He was looked on as being the elder statesman of German music and he will be remembered primarily for encouraging many bands like Kraftwerk to forge their own European identity.

Back in 1975, armed with this identity, the single of "Autobahn" had definitely put Kraftwerk on the musical map in a position of some authority. Can had proved some years earlier that commercial success could come out of improvisation with the single "Spoon". Kraftwerk had now proved with their synthetic version of a trip on a motorway that synthesizer music was workable, not only over the whole side of an LP, but also within the confines of a pop single. Today, although the track inevitably has a nostalgic feel to it, it still retains its resonance. It also remains a firm live favourite of the group and their fans, and somehow a Kraftwerk set without it would seem incomplete. The group were quick to realise that the LP was somewhat of a watershed in their career. Today, they don't play any pieces from the period prior to *Autobahn* on stage. Schneider now chooses to describe the early period prior to its release as "history – archeology".[22]

TRANSISTORS
and
URANIUM

THE SUDDEN IMPACT OF THE COMMERCIAL AND CRITICAL ACCLAIM that greeted the *Autobahn* album was obviously going to be a tough act to follow, even for a band as calculating and conceptual as Kraftwerk. Nonetheless, after their 1975 tour and the success of the LP and single, Kraftwerk set about recording a follow-up. The considerable amount of money they had made from their new-found commercial success wasn't frittered away, but ploughed back into updating their studio and equipment, so by the end of 1975 the first fully fledged incarnation of the studio had been completed.

This meant they could now record all their material at the Kling Klang studio and they no longer had to rely on outside producers or engineers. So, despite Conny Plank's feeling that he had been dropped by the group, it was probable that they no longer needed his services. Also, after the fluctuations in line-ups that accompanied previous LPs, the continued involvement of Flur and Bartos meant that the group now had some much needed stability and they could approach recording more as an established group.

From the very beginnings in 1970 they had always been able to rely on financial security which enabled them to constantly upgrade their own studio with the latest available technology. This obviously had positive advantages in terms of increased independence, as it meant that Hütter and Schneider could dictate their own terms. Florian Schneider:

"We have invested in our machines, we have enough money to live, that's it. We can do what we want, we are independent, we don't do cola adverts, even if we might have been flattered by such proposals, we never accepted."[1]

But on the negative side, such stability can also lead to complacency. Karl Bartos:

"If you are financially independent and you have this chemistry within the group it makes you very strong. But on the other side of the coin it makes you lazy. If you are from a working class background, you have to go to the studio and do three records a year.

Equipment was never a problem, buying a new synthesizer or whatever. The good thing about being rich is that it makes you independent, you don't have to be part of the music business where everybody lives off you. You just deliver a tape whenever you want."[2]

However, far from equipment being purchased on a whim, it was treated like a structured company re-investment programme. It exemplified the workmanlike way that the group were building on their success, treating the band, the recorded output and the studio as an identifiable whole that was essentially a business like any other. As Hütter was later to quip, "We are not artists nor musicians. First of all we are workers."[3]

Having said that, it was becoming clear that despite Hütter's claim, they were in fact rather more talented musicians than they cared to let on. It is unlikely that mere engineers or sound researchers would have been able to perfect the sorts of rhythms and melodies that the group were beginning to create. "Workers" undoubtedly would have continued in the far more rarified atmosphere of contemporary experimental music and not have entered into the much more competitive world of pop.

For their next LP, they decided that there should be a central theme or concept cementing it together. Hütter and Schneider had for a while been fascinated by the concept of communication, so they suggested to Schult that they do something based around radios. Their interest in radio communication had been enhanced during their first US tour which had included an interview circuit of college radio stations. In their typically conceptual way of looking at things, broadcasting from frequency to frequency across the States, they viewed themselves almost as a radio station in their own right. In any event, that summer Schult set up a temporary studio in one of Schneider's father's houses in Düsseldorf and started working on the graphics and some basic ideas for possible lyrics.

On the musical side of things, *Autobahn*'s successor did at least partially return them to the more avant-garde end of the spectrum. Called *Radio-Activity* (Radio-Aktivität), it was not only their first LP made with a healthy advance from their new deal with the EMI group, but also the first to appear in two different language versions – a German one released in November 1975 and an English one in January 1976. Being totally conceived and recorded in their own studio without the guiding hand of a co-producer, some might say that the resulting record was perhaps a little too conceptually clever-clever for its own good.

The cover returned to the Warholian principle of a simple object just like the earlier traffic cone. *Radio-Activity*'s cover was a clear visual pun on its title in portraying a single object – the front and back of a radio on the corresponding front and back covers. In direct juxtaposition to the modern shape of the music and to the implications of the nuclear title, the image was of an old German radio from the thirties. This was to become a regular trick in the Kraftwerk arsenal, of simultaneously playing about with the modernity and nostalgia of their imagery. They still regularly accompany the newness of their musical ideas with the romanticism of images, pictures and industrial design from a bygone age, thereby tugging the listener in two directions. Typical of their increasingly meticulous way of working, much time was spent on the cover. Emil Schult:

"I did about 10 or 15 front covers before the final one was done, and I drove around with Ralf in the Volkswagen all over the place to try and find the old radio for the back cover. It was fun, it was a nice summer."[4]

The radio that they eventually settled on was a shortwave one with a reception of a mere 200 kms. In fact it was a radio of the type which Goebbels had developed during the war so people wouldn't be subject to propaganda from further afield. Whether the group were aware of this at the time is uncertain. After the record's success in France they gave the original to their French label manager Maxime Schmitt who happened to come across one exactly similar in all but one feature in a Paris flea market, the only difference being a swastika between the volume and tuning dials. Not surprisingly, for the front cover of *Radio-Activity* they had either removed the swastika, or more probably it had been removed before they bought it.

On the inner sleeve, the four Kraftwerk members posed in their new uniform of grey or black suits reflecting the short-haired "classical quartet" image adopted for their American tour. As the *Trouser Press Record Guide* put it, "*Radio-Activity* coincided with a change of image that sliced away beards and hair and converted Kraftwerk from noodling hippies into ultramodern sonic engineers."[5] Schneider, almost shy in appearance, stands in front of some unidentifiable instrument (a kind of electric flute that looks like a neon tube), whilst Flur and Bartos seem amused at their electronic percussion drumsticks/mallets which look like strange knitting needles. It seems that Schneider was mostly responsible for the building of many of these mysterious instruments. Karl Bartos:

> "This electric drum machine took about two years to be achieved. The very first one was built by Florian out of an old organ beat box which he pulled apart and added the possibility of playing it by hand. The early drums were really like a closed circuit. If you have a connection between a piece of metal and a metal stick, as soon as you hit the metal with the stick you close an electric circuit and you are able to trigger a sound. Later on these were modified by engineers."[6]

For the front of the inner sleeve, Hütter adopts a studious pose with an old 30's microphone, harking back to the same period as the radio. The whole effect gives the group the look of four cottage industry instrument makers, from a time unrelated to any pop music fashion or trend. On the reverse of the inner sleeve there is a large drawing of an iron pylon, looking like the top section of the Eiffel Tower with an antenna on top. The radio antenna emits four waves symbolizing a pre-TV era when radio was the primary medium of mass communication.

In the lower right hand corner, there is a photograph of Emil Schult with long hair and a grey suit, holding what looks like pencils, a brush and a screwdriver, appearing to be the architect of the cover's concept and is indeed credited with the artwork. Together with Hütter and Schneider, he is also credited with a contribution to the lyrics of some of the tracks.

Musically, the LP itself was constructed a bit like an epic poem devoted to the age of electronic and nuclear power. By doing so, they were returning to the industrial fascinations that had proliferated earlier LPs. The important difference being, that whilst the early industrial sounds were aggressive and unfettered, by *Radio-Activity* they had been completely tamed to produce a sort of electronic chamber music.

Although mimicking the standard pop album and appearing to be constructed of 12 pieces of music (6 a side), there are in reality only two pop songs on the LP. These are "Radio Activity" and "Antenna" which respectively formed the A and B sides of a single. The single, although a hit in some countries including France, failed to follow the success of "Autobahn" in either the UK or the USA.

Whilst the cover of *Radio-Activity* alluded to radio communication, the track "Radio-Activity" clearly had nuclear implications more consistent with its title. By tackling a nuclear theme, Kraftwerk were reflecting a current political concern. By the mid-'70s the anti-nuclear movement was gaining ground and young people in particular were becoming concerned about ecology and the environment. Nowhere more so than in Germany, where the Green Party (Die Grünen) were making notable inroads into the mainstream of German politics, proliferating stickers with the message, "Atom Kraft – Nein Danke" (Nuclear Power – No Thanks).

However, many people missed the irony of the lyric to "Radio-Activity" which on first listening, appeared to sing its praises, with "it's in the air for you and me". The lyric has a romantic mood about it, like an unexpected updated version of *Tristan and Isolde*. In fact, it was intended as a humourous denunciation of nuclear power. Inevitably it was misinterpreted by those unable to see further than the surface, accusing Kraftwerk of being flippantly at odds with German youth. Not for the last time, some journalists wrongly surmised that Kraftwerk were trying to poke fun at people.

This impression probably wasn't helped by the fact that the group had even gone as far as having a promotional photograph taken of them visiting an atomic power plant in the Netherlands. The now familiar image shows the four members posing by some sort of reactor wearing white coats, gloves and large protective over-shoes. Whilst continuing their allusions to being laboratory technicians of a sort, it could have added to people's impression that they were endorsing nuclear power. It was a decision that could in retrospect be considered unwise.

However, this was of no concern to one of the great chroniclers of German obsessions, Rainer Werner Fassbinder who was impressed enough to use parts of the *Radio-Activity* album for his projects *Chinesiches Roulette* and *Berlin Alexanderplatz*. The latter used passages of Kraftwerk's music in the final apocalyptic dream sequence. In fact, in keeping with Fassbinder's obsessive life, his interest in Kraftwerk became rather more than that of a fan. Karl Bartos:

> "Fassbinder loved it. True there had been Can and Tangerine Dream, but Kraftwerk was the only pop band with the ability to do a three minute pop song with its own German identity. Fassbinder's crew were sometimes forced to listen to Kraftwerk eight hours a day on the set. He would play *Autobahn* and *Radio-Activity* to the point where no-one could stand it anymore. It was a bit like brain washing. Flattering to hear, though."[7]

However, the admiration was obviously mutual. The Kling Klang studio had a living room where the group would often sit and watch TV or listen to records by their favourite groups like The Beach Boys and The Kinks. Of an evening, they would quite often take a break from their recording to watch Fassbinder movies. The German film-maker was in some ways a kindred spirit, in that he was using film to reflect some very specific German post-war concerns just like Kraftwerk were doing musically.

The six themes on the first side of *Radio-Activity* are all linked together. "Geiger Counter" consists of simple thud which is accompanied by the noise of static. Such was the effect that when people first played the LP they thought that it was scratched or even that their equipment wasn't working. This then leads into "Radio-Activity" with its catchy, whistleable theme which could conceivably be described as the group's first attempt to write a fully fledged electronic pop song, and is notable as the first song the group also recorded in English.

"Radioland" has a slow tempo and minimal tune accompanied by a wavering oscillator, approximating the sound of someone quickly spinning the dial of a radio. The piece is a monotonous chant being essentially a duet between Hütter and Schneider singing two stanzas each alternately. They are joined in the last verse by a synthetic voice.

Next up is "Airwaves" which begins with an eery oscillator sound and is followed by an upbeat piece which alternates a synthesizer tune with a simple melody sung in harmony. They later used a similar mood on songs like "Metropolis" and "Neon Lights" from the *Man Machine* album.

"Intermission" is portrayed by a small radio type jingle followed by few moments of silence and what sounds like time pips. Although very Warhol-like in its statement of ultimate minimality, it was not unique in that John Lennon and Yoko Ono had already produced the rather longer "Two Minutes Of Silence". Similarly John Cage had "composed" an even longer piece of silence for the piano called "4.33" – which when recently made available as a CD single, must be the ultimate punchline to this particular joke. Side one ends with "News" which uses snippets of various news broadcasts mixed together until no particular voice is distinguishable.

"The Voice of Energy" which opens side two, anticipates the advent of Kraftwerk's robot voice. It is exactly the same treated vocal effect they would use to introduce the band's later concerts. This is followed by "Antenna" which is an often neglected but nonetheless influential Kraftwerk piece in that for the first time they were attempting to capture some of the spirit of rock 'n' roll music. Hütter's echoed vocal sounds like a precursor to Alan Vega's early LPs with Suicide. However, despite the track's potential it has never been played live.

Based around the same theme as "Radioland", "Radio Stars" features a background of a naggingly annoying oscillator, over which Hutter sings one line, then Schneider, then an arpeggiated vocoded vocal. The three voices mix themselves more and more, finally form a sort of cannon – half human, half mechanical. Following on, "Uranium" has a background choral effect, echoing the nuclear theme of "Radio-Activity", with the robotic "Voice Of Energy" providing an eery spoken vocal, whilst "Transistor" has a synthesizer tune somewhat similar to bagpipes and is a brief return to the electric piano sounds of the *Ralf and Florian* LP.

The album closes with "Ohm Sweet Ohm", which as well as being a humorous play on words, also uses the same formula as "Kometenmelodie 1 & 2" from the *Autobahn* LP. The mellotron and vocoded voices play a simple lullaby-like tune which speeds up. It is almost a post-apocalyptic theme for after the radioactive explosion.

In the classic terms of a follow up album, *Radio-Activity* was a relative flop in the bigger established markets of the UK and the USA. On its release it failed to chart in the UK, and following *Autobahn*'s top ten placing, it only reached a disappointing number 140 in the US charts. In some countries it had obviously served to confuse newly won critics and public alike as to exactly what sort of group Kraftwerk were. However, it wasn't all doom and gloom, as it was this LP that really opened up the European market for them, particularly in France where they received a gold disc for topping 100,000 sales (a figure which has subsequently doubled). Emil Schult:

> "*Radio-Activity* became very popular in France, and we tended to concentrate on this area. We did a lot of concerts in France. It was also the time that record companies and publishers started to become really interested in our music. Actually the new electronic music scene had started to come alive. We had initiated something with our first little home-built equipment, then people started to want to have it, everybody wanted a Moog synthesizer."[8]

A good deal of the record's success in France must be put down to Maxime Schmitt who, as Capitol's label manager at Pathé-Marconi, was given the job of promoting Kraftwerk to the French public. He had been aware of the "Autobahn" single as a one-off jukebox hit, but on hearing the *Radio-Activity* album he was completely won over by the music. This was further enhanced when he was introduced to the group by Paul Alessandrini at a concert in Lille. Like Schult he soon became a close confidant and adviser to the group. Maxime Schmitt:

> "I was immediately fascinated by the construction of the songs which is exactly what I loved in the construction of rock. It made me remember

The Beach Boys, The Shadows, but with an extra dimension that was completely new. It was a sort of modern equivalent of Elvis Presley. When people first heard Elvis it was like something they had not heard before. For me, Kraftwerk was something completely new. And I became more than a number one fan, I became involved with the group. The fact that my name sounds German was important. For them it was not a problem at all if my name appeared on the LP covers. If my name had been Boulanger or Meunier, it would have been embarassing to them – it would have bothered them."[9]

Schmitt was successful in persuading people in France that Kraftwerk's music was an important step in the development of pop and rock music, and that there was much more to the group than just "Autobahn". Being less concerned with the conceptual nature of the LP, Schmitt was convinced that the track "Radio-Activity" was a potential hit single. As a result, he managed to win over Jean-Loup Laffont at the *Europe 1* radio station who adopted the track as a signature tune for his programme. The single went on to become a summer hit in 1976 and sold a million copies in France. In December of that year, *Europe 1* voted *Radio-Activity* as their LP of the year. Maxime Schmitt:

"For me, Kraftwerk were typically rock. I had enough time to explain to people that the band was playing pop music. Without the public understanding this, I don't think it would ever have happened for the group. For instance, the two percussionists beating a rhythm with their knitting needles on pieces of iron. There was an energy emanating from that which was very unexpected – it was like Jerry Lee Lewis hammering away at his piano."[10]

Soon, Schmitt became a member of a select inner circle of people that would meet Kraftwerk at places like *La Coupole* restaurant in Paris. In fact, their reputation in France was now big enough that movie directors, artists and musicians were all queueing up to pay court to the mysterious German group that had suddenly usurped the artistic community's attention.

Gallic recognition aside, although having its pop moments, in other markets *Radio-Activity* was probably conceptually too dense and cluttered compared to either the hypnotic *Autobahn* or the streamlined pop of subsequent LPs. Although there were now clear signs of the Kraftwerk sardonic wit, this was seemingly only detectable to the French and those already initiated in the group's conceptual thinking. In the mainstream British or American markets, where they didn't have someone like Schmitt to push their music, much of *Radio-Activity*'s noises and bleeps were too difficult for mass consumption.

It is unclear whether they were really trying to be experimental again, or just expanding people's perception of pop music. They may well have thought it was important to confuse their new public by introducing them to something more complex, having got a foot in the door with the success of the "Autobahn" single. In reality, of course, many people were probably just expecting *"Autobahn 2"*, and as such were disappointed.

Although *Radio-Activity* was not received with the same universal reaction that had greeted the release of *Autobahn*, the group themselves seemed relatively undeterred. To promote the new LP, they made a promotional video clip with Günther Fröhling, a Düsseldorf based film-maker who went on to become a successful in TV commercials whilst remaining a close collaborator of the group. They also played some European dates including well-received shows at the Paris Olympia in February 1976. The whole mood of the concerts had a very German expressionist feel to them, evoking movies like "The Cabinet of Doctor Caligari".

Once again, Emil Schult had designed a stage set for the group. This was a starkly minimal presentation based around four neon signs with the first names of the group on them. Gone was the mass of tangled wires and cables that had proliferated at earlier concerts. Now, all the cables and plugs were hidden, giving a clean, bare appearance. This, coupled with the formal suits that the group were now wearing, completed the transformation.

The typical set of this period began with "Ruckzuck" from the first LP which they continued to play as it was an ideal way for the group to tune their instruments. Following on was "Kometenmelodie 1 & 2", "Tanzmuzik", "Radio-Activity" and "Airwaves". Lastly was a full length version of "Autobahn", often lasting up to half an hour, now confidently played with a newly found mastery and skill. They were also accompanying their set with a light and slide show which was growing in sophistication.

For an encore the group sometimes featured an instrumental which included themes from "Radio-Activity", and also the birth of a melody which was later to become "Showroom Dummies". The piece seemed more or less improvised and showed that the group remained unafraid to compose and improvise on stage. The presence of themes from past and future recordings would seem to bear out Hütter's assertions on various occasions that each new piece was born out of the old ones, comparing it to branches of a tree that grow, divide and recreate themselves.

It would be easy to criticize these concerts, especially in the light of the hi-tech professional shows that the group now put on. However, although the pieces were often prone to self-indulgence, it was somehow consistent with their past that they were still prepared to take risks on stage. Certainly, it was often hard for audiences to grasp their attempts to reproduce their studio sound, and onlookers were often surprised at the difference between the recorded version and its live equivalent. This is in stark contrast to today, where there is little difference between recorded and live versions.

It is now easily forgotten that during a performance, Kraftwerk could sometimes be subtle and effective improvisers. In fact, by 1976 there were few groups from the early German improvising scene left with much credibility. Kraftwerk were now alone in having distanced themselves from the hippyish and nonsensical aspects of Kraut Rock, and their live shows were becoming recognised as something out of the ordinary and unique. For one thing, the atmosphere backstage was vastly different to that of the normal rock concert with its drug taking and hangers on. Backstage at a Kraftwerk gig was, then as now, very serious and business-like, with the group being very tidy and technically precise with their machines. Emil Schult was even spotted wearing white gloves – possibly so as not to damage the equipment – but inevitably it helped to give the backstage area the feeling of a laboratory. It was soon clear that being a member of Kraftwerk implied adhering to a high level of discipline. Karl Bartos:

"We had certain rules, like we wouldn't get drunk at parties, or drunk on stage of course – because it is not easy to turn the knobs on a synthesizer if you are drunk or full of drugs. So, that was a kind of rule, but we never talked about it. We always tried to keep very aware of what we were doing while we were acting in public... Not that I have anything against getting drunk you understand!"[11]

The combination of the adventurous *Radio-Activity* LP and the unpredictable nature of their live shows, meant that outside France people were inevitably dismissing the success of *Autobahn* as a 'one off' – a sort of European oddity. Clearly, critics were wrong to try and shrug them off so easily. But in response, whatever avant-garde experimentation the group indulged in from now on was kept firmly within the walls of the Kling Klang studio. The future, on record and live, would be far more firmly rooted toward electronic pop tunes. However, they never completely abandoned using experimental noises in their music – somehow always retaining that innovative edge.

As 1976 turned into 1977, it was clear that punk music was going to hijack the record business at gun point. Kraftwerk, with deft timing, conveniently dropped from their live performances the last vestiges of the early '70's musical freedom and improvisation – just the sort of thing that some of the punk bands were apparently kicking so hard against. However, it should be noted that many of these bands like The Buzzcocks and Siouxsie and the Banshees identified with the anarchy of some of the early '70s German bands, and often cited groups like Can, Faust and Kraftwerk as influences.

TRANS-EUROPE EXPRESS

TRAINS
and
EUROPE

BY MID-1976 KRAFTWERK WERE ALREADY HARD AT WORK ON THEIR next LP. It was, not surprisingly, recorded at the Kling Klang studio in Düsseldorf, but perhaps in order to avoid the introspection of *Radio-Activity*, Hütter and Schneider decided to visit California that summer and mix the tracks at the famous Record Plant Studio in Los Angeles. In general they found the cultural and geographical distance from Germany a stimulating atmosphere in which to work. It is perhaps ironic that they put the finishing touches to their most conceptually European LP on the West Coast of the USA. An oblique comparison might be drawn with Fritz Lang who utilised the cinematic expertise of Hollywood to create movies that were full of expressionist references to German culture and its poetic vision of reality.

During their trip to America, Hütter and Schneider took the opportunity to see The Beach Boys on their home territory playing in a big stadium. They were suitably impressed by their erstwhile idols. Hütter even commented, "There is a wonderful song on their new album called "Once In My Life". I would like to say once in my own life all the things that Brian Wilson says in this song."[1]

By the end of 1976 they had also been given an unexpected boost by David Bowie, who had become an unofficial publicist for the group. During his *Station To Station* tour, he had preceded his performances with tapes that were almost exclusively made up of music by Kraftwerk. Initially, Hütter and Schneider had been offered the opportunity to play the support slot on the tour. It must have been surprising to anyone not aware of Kraftwerk's increasing ambivalence to such offers, that they turned down what was in effect a golden opportunity to appear before millions of people.

In fact, they had always played live on their own terms. With the exception of the German Music Festival in Paris, they had steered clear of playing alongside other groups. In the end, with Bowie's patronage they almost achieved the same result as if they had accepted the support slot, since millions of people heard the group's work on tape. This may well have given Hütter the first inkling of an idea that the group were later to cherish as a future possibility – that of touring without ever leaving Düsseldorf.

It is more likely that the group didn't actually say "No" to Bowie but more characteristically the offer was probably never answered. In reality the group were genuinely concerned that with Bowie's attentions they might appear more like his protégés, instead of one of his influences. In any event, this was the first of many subsequent refusals (or lack of response) to participate in high profile live work, collaboration or production projects.

By the end of his "Thin White Duke" tour, Bowie was looking for the inspiration to make another of his familiar chameleon-like changes. Somewhat surprisingly, he looked toward Germany. Deserting his cocaine-fuelled lifestyle in Hollywood, he upped and relocated to West Berlin where, in a short space of frantic and awe-inspiring creativity, he would record his next three solo LPs – certainly amongst his best music – as well as producing two classic LPs for Iggy Pop.

In searching for a new sound to accompany his new choice of home, Bowie inevitably rediscovered old LPs by Cluster, Neu! and Kraftwerk. The balance between improvisation and cyclical structures obviously impressed him, being clearly visible on the first of his German trilogy released in January 1977. *Low*, like its successor *Heroes*, was recorded with fellow conceptualist and general all-round rock non-conformist Brian Eno. *Heroes* even featured a track apparently dedicated to Kraftwerk entitled "V2 Schneider".

Despite Bowie now living in Berlin, he and Kraftwerk had not actually crossed paths. A meeting had been scheduled for the autumn of 1976 but was cancelled due to Kraftwerk's touring commitments following the release of *Radio-Activity*. It was clear that Hütter and Schneider were flattered by the attention that Bowie was giving them and that their respect for him was mutual – especially as he was now recording with Iggy Pop, the former lead singer of one of their favourite bands The Stooges. In *Rock & Folk* magazine, Hütter described to Paul Alessandrini how they had first met Iggy Pop in a lift. He explained that he had always liked the daring approach of The Stooges which had reminded him of his days as a student participating in various happenings in the late sixties.

Hütter also mentioned in an interview that Bowie and Kraftwerk would be recording together when Bowie next visited Düsseldorf. The recording session never materialised, but they did eventually meet, marking the beginning of an ongoing friendship that saw Bowie visiting Hütter and Schneider at the Kling Klang studio. However, these visits were presumably none too regular, or relatively low-key, as neither Bartos or Flur were ever given the opportunity to meet Bowie.

Legend has it that on his first encounter with Hütter and Schneider, Bowie had been playing *Autobahn* in his Mercedes and commented on how effectively it conjured up driving on German roads. Schneider apparently remarked in return that they had experienced a similar sensation when they had visited California and found that driving on the West Coast was exactly the feeling evoked by The Beach Boys.

Mutual appreciation aside, how close Kraftwerk and Bowie were to actually collaborating musically is uncertain. It would undoubtedly have been a very unusual step for Kraftwerk to take, given that they had never visibly collaborated with anyone else outside of the Kraftwerk family. Suffice to say, it is probable that Bowie would have benefited more from such a collaboration, just as he had seemed to gain strength from working with Mick Ronson, Lou Reed, Eno and Fripp, Iggy Pop and later on Nile Rodgers.

Nevertheless, rumours abounded about various rendezvous in German coffee shops, where Bowie and Kraftwerk would discuss European issues, German technology, futurism and philosophy. Whether these were reality or mythology is a bit blurred by the mists of time, but for a while the two parties did meet on a fairly regular basis. Maxime Schmitt:

"I remember one meeting. It was in Paris, after one of Bowie's concerts. He had hired the *L'ange Bleu* nightclub on the Champs-Elysées for a private party. When we arrived there was Bowie, Iggy Pop and their court, and when Ralf and Florian walked in they received a five minute standing ovation. Iggy Pop was gazing devotedly at them, he completely adored them. Both he and Bowie were transfixed, Bowie was saying to Iggy Pop, "Look how they are, they are fantastic!"[2]

Despite Kraftwerk's worries that Bowie was merely interested in cultivating them as a backing band, the association didn't seem to do either artist any harm. Certainly Bowie's music of the late '70s seemed to benefit from the coldness and inventiveness of Kraftwerk, while in return perhaps Kraftwerk's own work in some way benefited from the warmth of Bowie and Iggy Pop's material. In the end, music from both Kraftwerk and Bowie appeared alongside each other in Chris Petit's late '70s road movie *Radio On*.

Later, although apparently remaining friends, Kraftwerk and Bowie grew apart when Bowie moved on from his arty conceptual German trilogy back to making more conventional pop music. Later, he even apparently went on to describe Kraftwerk's music as too wise.

However, as a result of the connection between Bowie and Kraftwerk, Hütter and Schneider became friends with Kuêlan, who Bowie and Iggy Pop had written about in the song "China Girl". The group would often visit her in Paris where she still lives with a famous French rock singer. She is still in contact with the group and Schneider in particular. Kuêlan:

"When they came to Paris they liked to stay at the Royal Monceau Hotel. I would go with them to exhibitions, museums, in fact they made me discover a Paris which I didn't know. One day, I remember we went to the Musée de la Presse (the Press Museum) which is in Les Halles and we stayed there all afternoon. They wanted to look at all the French press of the 1930s and they analysed everything. They seemed to be very reflective about the subject.

They were like tourists, only very refined ones. They were like the cream of the tourists. We went to movies and exhibitions, and they especially liked to go to the famous *Le Sept* bar where they would meet up with friends of Andy Warhol."[3]

The results of Kraftwerk's European attitude and their subsequent mixing on the West Coast, surfaced on their 1977 LP *Trans-Europe Express*. In fact, by the time the LP was released some of the elements of the US mix had been dropped, most notably more upfront vocals, in favour of further mixing that had been done in Hamburg and Düsseldorf. *Trans-Europe Express* was eventually released between Bowie's *Low* and *Heroes*, and with its overwhelmingly European feel it could definitely be said to fall into a similar musical vein.

However, as an LP it was far removed from the revolution happening with the emergence of punk, and therefore worlds apart from what was perceived as "new". 1977 was a watershed year, as punk had devastatingly usurped everyone's attention. As a result a whole range of attitudes, conventions and staid practices were being challenged. In Britain and America, punk rock turned everything on its head, albeit briefly, as record executives scampered around their corporate corridors like headless chickens, trying to react to what was a potential revolution in the making. In the end, it was a revolution that partially backfired, as record companies learned all too quickly to embrace and coerce punk into their way of thinking. However, as a spirit of rejuvenation, its legacy is still reverberating today.

Punk was very much based around the sound of thrashing guitars and drums – a return to a more basic approach toward rock 'n' roll. Not surprisingly, *Trans-Europe Express* displayed no such return to basic instrumentation. In a lot of ways, the futurist course that the group had now truly set themselves was at direct odds with the "no future" mentality of many of the punk bands. So, whilst most people's attentions were drawn to the Sex Pistols and The Clash, musicians like Kraftwerk, Bowie and Eno were now almost forcibly working within a vacuum partly of their own making, but also partly due to the large rift that had now opened up in the music business.

This rift was now clearly perceived as being between the progressive rock groups of the early '70s, who were now considered to be musical dinosaurs lumbering around the world with expensive and mostly self-defeating stage shows, and the brash and angry punk bands. Musicality was out – now in fashion was loud, aggressive, anarchic music. Being able to play an instrument properly was a secondary consideration, if one at all.

Kraftwerk were clearly apart from either of these camps, having carved out a niche somewhere in the middle. Having severed their contacts with progressive rock they had thereby retained some of the credibility that had been lost by the dinosaur bands. However, by not visibly adopting any punk stance they could not by any stretch of the imagination be associated with the burgeoning 'New Wave'.

The tag 'New Wave' was in reality a strange paradox. In fact, punk had only thrown up a limited number of truly original bands with a new approach toward music. Most punk bands were only new in adopting a sneering, irreverent attitude toward business and authority. Much of the music was merely a throwback to '60s groups like The Seeds, The Stooges, The Pretty Things and the early Rolling Stones. The furore that surrounded punk with its safety pins and bondage trousers left Kraftwerk in the somewhat ironic position of being seen as "old fashioned", although this misconception may have had more to do with their formal clothes than their music.

This isolation probably suited them just fine. There was already a certain mystique and uniqueness building up around the group from Düsseldorf which the split between punk and progressive rock only served to further intensify. Increasingly, they adopted a stance beyond that of a normal rock group, whether it was New Wave or Old Wave. It was almost as if they had barricaded themselves inside their Kling Klang studio, building up a wall of silence against the outside world, appearing oblivious to any musical trend but their own.

However, it would be misleading to give the impression that Kraftwerk were unaware of, or unresponsive to trends within the music business. Of all the emerging punk groups they were most impressed by The Ramones, who had continued the US guitar-saturated tradition of The Stooges and the MC5. The Ramones had, like Kraftwerk, adopted a kind of corporate image, with each member being called Ramone. Also, they had a type of uniform, albeit rather basic, of black leather jackets, white T-shirts and ripped jeans.

The front cover of *Trans-Europe Express* was in an oblique way influenced by the sleeve of the first Ramones LP which had been released in 1976. Originally, Kraftwerk's new LP was to have a rather lavish colour cover, but in the end they reverted to using black and white. This reflected the more down-to-earth approach of punk bands' album covers, and not the flamboyant artwork still being used by established rock bands.

The artwork was originally intended to be based around "The Hall Of Mirrors", with the reflections of all four members in a series of mirrors. However, this may well have been dropped due to its similarity to Fripp and Eno's cover to their *No Pussyfooting* LP released in 1972. In the end the sleeve to *Trans-Europe Express* features a heavily touched-up photo by Maurice Seymour in New York, with the four members almost indistinguishable from mannequins dressed in suits. This rather old-fashioned image was once again in stark contrast to the modern sheen of the music. Similarly, the other photograph by J. Stara in Paris shows the group continuing the classical string quartet image that Hütter had created. By accident or design, for the US release of the LP not only were these two photos reversed with the colour photo appearing on the front, but the photo itself was printed the wrong way round.

The idea of rather stiff and inanimate posing in photographs may well have been inspired once again by Warhol's idea of the artist as product, but there are also certain intense similarities with the perfomance art of Gilbert & George. The art duo would often stand for hours on end in tweed suits, with gold or red painted faces, posing as living sculptures at various installations. In one notable performance in 1970 called *The Singing Sculpture*, they did a version of "Underneath The Arches" for eight hours on two consecutive days in Kraftwerk's hometown at the Düsseldorf Kunsthalle.

On the inside sleeve of *Trans-Europe Express*, the four adopt another of their own frozen poses, sitting at a small square table with a checkered tablecloth, whilst behind them is a backcloth painting of a typical Bavarian scene. Apart from the absence of steins of beer, to all intents and purposes it was Kraftwerk "go on a picnic" – or almost as if posing as cardboard cut out extras for a scene in the film *Cabaret*. Other shots from the same photo session which had been taken on their US tour, show the group in a highly jocular mood, laughing and smiling, but these were presumably deemed as being too flippant to use.

Despite promoting a "non smiling" exterior image, it was obvious that by now the group were not quite the po-faced experimentalists that some had portrayed. They were patently enjoying playing about with the image they presented to the public. Much of this playfulness and wry sense of humour was now evident through their artwork. Anyone who still saw Kraftwerk as totally serious was partly missing the point.

However, a measure of how studiously they thought about what was included on their covers is given by Maxime Schmitt:

> "I remember on the sleeve, they were very embarrassed about the appearance of the word Rüssl (as in Rüssl Studio where some of the mixing was done). In German the word Rüssel means the trunk of an elephant or the snout of a pig. They thought that this name didn't fit in with the other words on the LP like Record Plant and Kling Klang... They were always careful about these sorts of things."[4]

Incidentally, there are a host of name credits on the LP including Maxime Schmitt, Emil Schult, Paul Alessandrini and Peter Bollig. Emil Schult was responsible for the little cartoons that depicted each track on the inside sleeve, similar to those he had done for the *Ralf and Florian* LP. Bollig is credited as an engineer, a title which extended to his role as the restorer of Hütter and Schneider's collection of Mercedes cars. He was responsible for many of the finishing touches like replacing the curtain over the back window or finding the Mercedes badge to go in the centre of the steering wheel. Alessandrini was credited as he was partially responsible for giving the LP its concept. Paul Alessandrini:

> "We were trying to think of somewhere to have lunch. I suggested *Le Train Bleu* (a restaurant on the first floor of the Gare de Lyon building in Paris). It's at the station where trains leave for Lyons, Marseille, Italy, Switzerland, the Middle East etc. I knew that Ralf and Florian liked these kinds of restaurants a lot. There was Maxime, Ralf, Florian, my wife Marjorie, and me. We spoke a lot, whilst watching the trains which you can see leaving from the restaurant window. I remember saying to them, "With the kind of music you do, which is kind of like an electronic blues, railway stations and trains are very important in your universe, you should do a song about the Trans Europe Express." And that was why me and Marjorie were credited on the sleeve.

> With Kraftwerk there is an intellectual process which precedes the musical process. Their way of making music is very thoughtful, but the

result is very minimal. It reminds me of great painters like Klee, Mondrian or Picasso, who are great technicians but whose works are minimal."[5]

So, having started with an intensely conceptual approach to the nature of an LP, the group ensured that the musical end product reflected their interest in uncomplicated presentation. Ralf Hütter:

"Our music is rather minimalist. If we can convey an idea with one or two notes, it is better to do this than to play a hundred or so notes. With our musical machines, there is no question of playing with a kind of virtuosity, there is all the virtuosity we need in the machines, so we concentrated our work towards a very direct minimalism."[6]

After what some saw as the musical uncertainties of *Radio-Activity*, *Trans-Europe Express* was the natural successor to *Autobahn*'s anthem to the motorway, reflecting the group's fascination with modes of transport. The new LP's title track sang the praises of a trans-European rail network that crossed the barriers and borders of Europe. For this they recreated a whole railway universe from within their studio, using synthesizers and electronics to their full potential to recreate the evocative sounds of trains. Once again the group didn't have to look far for inspiration. Düsseldorf's central station was only a stone's throw away from their studio, and many of the old TEE network of trains used to pass through such as the Amsterdam to Switzerland express.

In a way, incorporating train noises was like an updated version of Arthur Honegger's symphonic poem "Pacific 231" composed in 1923 – a homage to a steam locomotive of the same name. The very same train cropped up again as one of the locomotives featured in Kraftwerk's live video accompaniment to "Trans-Europe Express".

Kraftwerk's own symphonic poem to train travel reflected the constant travelling between Germany, Paris and the South of France that the group now regularly undertook. These journeys, often by train as the group disliked flying, re-inforced the inspiration for the LP's concept. Maxime Schmitt:

"There was all this thing; the trunk road/Nationale 7, the Nationale 1, the European motorway, it was fantastic. I was rediscovering what I had found in Chuck Berry with "Route 66" or in the "Fun Fun Fun" of The

Beach Boys. The idea was really that Kraftwerk was a train which crosses Europe, and people get into the wagons as one goes along."[7]

Hütter and Schneider were rather taken with the image of a train as a metaphor for the group. Thus the Kraftwerk engine would roll across Europe, with Hütter in the role of driver and Schneider stoking the group's conceptual boilerhouse, stopping to pick up a couple of contributors for a few stations and then letting them off. This notion of transitory participants certainly helps to explain Hütter and Schneider's non-committal approach to fully incorporating Flur, Bartos and Schult into the Kraftwerk ethos. Also, like the autobahn, the train represented a form of industrial movement of the kind that had so captivated the group from the very beginning. Ralf Hütter:

"The movement fascinates us, instead of a static or motionless situation. All the dynamism of industrial life, of modern life. We really speak about our experiences, of life as it appears to us. Even the artistic world does not exist outside of daily life, it is not another planet, it is here on the Earth that things are happening."[8]

To continue the rail theme, for the release of the LP a rather extravagant train journey was planned for the press by EMI France. Karl Bartos:

"We had much fun during this period. I particularly remember this train trip that Maxime Schmitt organised for us for the launching of *Trans-Europe Express* in France. The record company had hired a train with old fashioned carriages from the thirties to travel from Paris to Rheims. The album was played to the journalists during the journey. By the time we arrived in Rheims and had visited one of the famous Champagne cellars all the journalists were drunk."[9]

Although *Trans-Europe Express* saw Bartos and Flur further entrenched in the Kraftwerk set up, their contribution was still confined to being credited with electronic percussion. However, the stability in line-up enabled Kraftwerk to build upon the impression of a corporate foursome working as a fully integrated group. Artistic control remained firmly under the guidance of Hütter and Schneider, who are credited with all the writing, (apart from Emil Schult who gets a joint lyric credit on "The Hall Of Mirrors" and the title track "Trans-Europe Express").

The name Kraftwerk now embodied more than just the production of music, it was a vehicle reflecting a way of life, and as such was something that they were now taking very seriously. It was becoming evident that there was much more to being a member of Kraftwerk than just playing music. It was more of an artistic lifestyle statement. As a result, the group and those close to them, regularly travelled, holidayed and generally hung out together. They visited London, New York and Paris, and were regular visitors to St Tropez, where the Schneider family owned a villa. Despite being on holiday and away from their Düsseldorf factory, much of the time was spent analysing their music and their approach to it. Karl Bartos:

> "Even on holiday we would talk about music, how we should go in this direction, or that direction. We would listen to the demo tapes as we drove around and we would decide if we needed more metal or more bass drum. It was a whole electronic lifestyle. Of course, we also rode bikes and went to the beach!"[10]

It was just such a holiday that the group took to the South of France with Emil Schult and Maxime Schmitt in the summer of 1976, whilst working on *Trans-Europe Express*. For relaxation, the group had now established the kind of routine that was indicative of the way they liked to operate – essentially doing the same things everyday. So, whilst at home in Düsseldorf they would go to the coffee house and then to the studio to work or relax, so on holiday they would drink coffee, ride bikes and go to the local discos in the evening. However, all four members of the group were careful not to sunbathe so as to retain the white, rather wan faces always apparent in publicity photographs and on album sleeves.

The *Trans-Europe Express* LP, released in May 1977, opens with "Europe Endless" which was at one time to have been the title of the LP. The track is a prophetic insight toward a Europe of open borders that can only have been a twinkling in the eye of even the most ardent pro-European at the time. This is followed by "Hall of Mirrors" which has a lyric opined in a deadpan voice ruminating about how stars view their image in a looking glass. Hütter and Schneider described the song as semi-autobiographical, maybe meaning that the group's identity was somehow unattainable – on the other side of the mirror.

Side one ends with "Showroom Dummies", re-inforcing the image on the front cover, an initial blueprint for the increasing fascination with presenting themselves as inaminate or robotic characters. The idea for the track had come from a review of the first Kraftwerk concert in the UK, where a journalist had written that Flur and Bartos looked like showroom dummies on stage.

The track was also recorded in English, and at Maxime Schmitt's suggestion in French. Called "Les Mannequins", it became as familiar as the original title. This was their first excursion singing in the French language, but a successful one which prompted them to record French versions of several future tracks. For some versions they added the spoken introduction of "ein zwei drei vier" as a parody of The Ramones, who started each track with "one two three four". "Showroom Dummies" was about as clear an indication as one could have hoped to get that Kraftwerk had now fully entered the pop music world – and as such clearly influenced many later synthesizer pop groups like Depeche Mode, whose early recordings are very similar to this track.

Side two opens with the title track "Trans-Europe Express" and to many, this is the LP's most powerfully memorable moment. This was also evident to the group themselves as they were persuaded by Schmitt to change the title of the LP accordingly. Similar to David Bowie's 1976 LP *Station To Station*, the track opens with a simulated or actual train noise. The repetitive rhythm of the train gives way to one of the group's funkiest drum beats so far, showing an increasing grasp and developing fascination with danceable beats. The lyric includes the line 'station to station' followed by the recounting of a meeting between the group, David Bowie and Iggy Pop, again echoing the influence the two parties were having on each other.

With the help of Günther Fröhling, the group made a promotional video clip which featured them on a train journey, not on the actual TEE, but on a return journey between Düsseldorf and neighbouring Duisburg. The group are filmed wearing long coats, looking like they have stepped out of a Fritz Lang film, or four people auditioning for the part of Harry Lime in "The Third Man". Photo stills from this video were later used on a limited edition 12" single of "Showroom Dummies".

The track "Trans-Europe Express" runs directly into "Metal on Metal" which concentrates on the powerfully metallic nature of the drumbeat to "Trans Europe Express" whilst the riff later sampled on "Planet Rock" by Afrika Bambaataa plays over the top. "Franz Schubert" is a fairly innocuous instrumental filler but a title which provided Hütter with one of his more humorous anecdotes, claiming that Franz Schubert had actually visited the studio when they were recording the track. Following on is the vocoded coda of "Endless Endless" which brings the LP full circle.

There were now clear indications that Kraftwerk had perfected the synthesis of pop music with the avant-garde sounds and concepts that had previously preoccupied them. As their first LP to totally achieve this goal, many felt *Trans-Europe Express* set a precedent and was perhaps the group's most important LP. Maxime Schmitt:

> "Everything started there. Today, if you hear the words Trans-Europe Express, you immediately think about Kraftwerk. For me, *Trans-Europe Express* is inevitably their finest record, even if there are beautiful songs on the other records. It is the perfect record, the perfect concept, a totally successful cover – I even think that soundwise it is one of the best records."[11]

Of course, today the TEE network doesn't exist anymore and we are now in the TGV era. The Kraftwerk piece therefore undoubtedly has a nostalgic air to it, conjuring up a time when the old trains had rather dream-like names such as "L'Etoile du Nord", "der Rheingold", "Le Cisalpin", or "Le Mistral".

Many avant-garde musicians and artists had for a long time strived to incorporate the sounds and images of industry into art. The Dadaists and Futurists of the 20's and 30's had emphasized the inclusion of everyday sounds and images in their art in an attempt to move outside the gallery establishment. In the 60's, many of the American avant-garde composers also tried to incorporate every conceivable notion of sound and redefine it in the context of music. However, the more they tried, the more elite and "arty" it seemed to become. Somehow they had marginalised the sounds, making them acceptable to the few 'in the know', whilst generally being viewed as cranky or just plain unlistenable by the masses.

Trans-Europe Express and its title track in particular, had found a disciplined and streamlined way of incorporating the sounds of everyday industry and transport into structures which were essentially pop songs. Just as Warhol had encapsulated the pop art movement with a few simple images, so Kraftwerk had captured the essence of electronic pop with their economy of synthesized sound. Tracks like "Trans-Europe Express" managed to evoke speed or machinery without creating complicated mechanical or machine-like concertos. Like Warhol's art which had been aimed at mass consumption, so Kraftwerk tackled the idea of creating an 'industrial' music within the framework of pop music, rather than producing it for an elite of avant-garde music fans.

Up to that time, it was without doubt Kraftwerk's most impressive LP, being rounded with a consistency of purpose and littered with memorable tunes. *Trans-Europe Express* avoided the impression of *Autobahn* and its predecessors, which could be considered as LPs with a central piece of music surrounded by rather superfluous extra tracks. Nor was it weighed down by the sometimes almost unwarranted avant-garde noises of *Radio-Activity*. The LP has a complete cohesion, the vocal lines are clear and decisive, the melodies simple and catchy.

Sales of *Trans-Europe Express* fared slightly better than *Radio-Activity*, reaching No 119 in the US charts. Later it re-entered the US charts at No 67 in June 1978, but it wasn't until February 1982 that the LP was better recognised after Afrika Bambaataa had sampled the title track, reaching No 49 in the UK charts. The title track has always remained a disco favourite, particularly in the US, where as recently as 1990 it was released as a single in the *Classic Capitol Dance Tracks* series.

In retrospect, *Trans-Europe Express* was indeed so far ahead of its time that it is not surprising that it took many people a while to appreciate its subtlety. Whilst many of the group's original fans may have seen the LP's electro-pop as a sell out, for many potential pop fans, who in 1977 were besotted by all things punk, it was quite simply too sophisticated. When electro-pop music came to mass acceptance in the 1980s, it was soon evident where it had all began.

Although many wouldn't appreciate Kraftwerk's achievement until much later, within punk there were a number of groups in England picking up on Kraftwerk's industrial ideas. By 1978, Throbbing Gristle and Cabaret Voltaire were the pioneers of a music that was to be termed 'industrial'. Throbbing Gristle started their own Industrial label in London to release the harsh noise warfare of their own music, whilst in their Sheffield studio called Western Works, Cabaret Voltaire used their own obsessions with black dance music to produce a haphazard mixture of industrial sounds and primitive drum machines with Burroughs' cut-ups. Both groups had continued in the German experimental tradition of establishing their own studios as a base to work from. As Richard H. Kirk from Cabaret Voltaire explains, "I think there were a lot of people in England who were into Kraftwerk, Can and the other German groups, but there was no other group in England putting that sort of thing together at that time."[12]

Similarly in America, guitar-based music wasn't having everything its own way. From within the early punk music scene in New York emerged the totally synthesized Suicide, who combined Alan Vega's manic and frightening Presley-obsessed delivery with Martin Rev's furiously throbbing backdrops of drum machine and synthesizer.

Kraftwerk had showed with tracks like "Metal on Metal" that the sounds of industry and the noise of the factory could be effectively incorporated within rock and pop music. Inevitably, other groups would latch onto the concept of these industrial rhythms. In the early '80s in Germany, DAF (German Robert Görl and Spaniard Gabi Delgado who had met in Düsseldorf) aided by Conny Plank, produced a highly sexed music from basic drum and synthesizer patterns. Likewise Berlin's Einstürzende Neubauten incorporated electric drills, bed springs and every conceivable appliance to build up an armoury of percussion. Also, Düsseldorf's Die Krupps, and Pyrolator from the Düsseldorf-based label Ata-tak, played around with industrial ideas. Similarly in Britain, Test Department used oil drums and metal containers to bash out metallic symphonies that almost seemed to have tunes of their own.

Although Kraftwerk themselves are now considerably removed from any industrial/noise element in their music, it is still a strain that exists today. Nitzer Ebb, Front 242, Nine Inch Nails and Laibach to name but a few groups who are continuing in the same "industrial" tradition whilst owing a huge debt to Kraftwerk.

With *Trans-Europe Express* Kraftwerk had completed the transformation into an electronic pop band. Having moved from the very German-influenced *Autobahn* and *Radio-Activity*, through to a more musically and spiritually European outlook, they were now ready to turn their attentions to producing a worldwide, global album. They were also poised to take their automaton image another important step forward.

MAN
and
MACHINE

BY 1978 THE PUNK REVOLUTION HAD NOW GIVEN WAY TO SOMETHING called New Wave, which embraced just about anyone who had cut out guitar solos and cut their hair. New Wave music saw the almost exclusively guitar-based punk music widen its horizons to incorporate other instruments such as keyboards and saxes – but not as yet the synthesizer, which was still mainly associated with the dinosaur rock bands. New Wave was altogether a much tamer beast than punk had been, and record companies breathed a sigh of relief with the advent of its more user-friendly power pop. As a tag, New Wave came to be mostly a misnoma, many of its exponents sounding remarkably similar to the old wave dinosaur bands – only with short hair.

Following on from the success of *Trans-Europe Express*, Kraftwerk were confident that it was they who were at the vanguard of a "new wave" of their own. Despite (or perhaps because of) their apparent isolation, their next LP precipitated the dawning of a new electronic pop age – so much so, that it would be impossible to ignore them as a seminal driving force in moving pop music forward. Released in May 1978, *Man Machine (Die Mensch Maschine)* was stunningly ahead of its time. Consistent with their policy of self-sufficiency, the LP was totally recorded at the Kling Klang studio, but due to its complexity it was mixed at the Studio Rudas in Düsseldorf. Karl Bartos:

"At that time we needed a bigger console than that which we had at the Kling Klang studio. The two mixing engineers were Joschko Rudas and a black guy called Leanard Jackson who we'd flown in from LA to do a few tracks. It was very cold that winter, and being from LA, it was not that easy for him."[1]

Leanard Jackson from Whitfield Records had arrived from America fully expecting to be assisting with a record by four black guys from Düsseldorf. Having listened to their music he was convinced that the basic rhythm tracks had to have been produced by black musicians. So, not only was he surprised by the severe temperatures, which went down to minus 17 degrees that particular winter, but also by the fact that he was working with four white musicians. Nevertheless, the mixing went well, despite the distraction of numerous snowball fights.

The cohesion that now existed within the group was reflected in the resulting music. After all, this was the fourth LP to feature Wolfgang Flur, and the third with Karl Bartos.

As the group developed and expanded their technology and equipment, exactly how they composed or delegated responsibilities within the confines of the Kling Klang studio became an increasingly intriguing question. Sometimes Hütter would deflect inquirers with oblique answers like, "We compose the melodies by humming in our studio, and the rhythm comes from the noises of the machines".[2] On other occasions he would be a bit more specific. Ralf Hütter:

"We make compositions from everything. All is permitted, there is no working principle, there is no system. Our ideas really come from our experience, "alltags" in German, everyday life. We are playing the machines, the machines play us, it is really the exchange and the friendship we have with the musical machines which make us build a new music."[3]

Karl Bartos, however, is more illuminating on exactly how the songs were composed:

"Very simply, somebody would do the introduction, someone else the coda, we would improvise – jamming together for two or three hours... Florian was a lot more involved with the texture of the sound and the machines, he's not what I would call a musician, he's more of an artist. He would alter the sound of the melodies – he is able to do crazy stuff. He doesn't know chords as such, his musical approach is rather oriental,

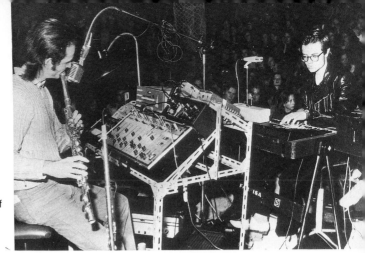

Top: An early Kraftwerk concert. (E. Koerner)

Middle: The group in Spring 1975. (Emil Schult)

Bottom: In the Pathé-Marconi office receiving a gold disc for sales of *Radioactivity* in France. Back row: Florian Schneider, Wolfgang Flur, Ralf Hütter and Karl Bartos. Front row: Emil Schult and Maxime Schmitt. (Jean-Luc Mabit)

Top left: Lunch with Paul Alessandrini and his wife where the concept for the *Trans-Europe Express* LP was born. (Patrick Jelin)

Middle and bottom left: The group at the Gare De L'Est in Paris prior to the promotional train trip to Rheims for the launch of *Trans-Europe Express,* and during the same trip. (Jean-Luc Mabit)

Top right: Paul Alessandrini, Florian Schneider and Ralf Hütter. (Patrick Jelin)

Bottom right: Ralf Hütter and Florian Schneider at an exhibition in Paris, appropriately called Les Machines Célibataires (The Batchelor Machines). (Jean-Luc Mabit)

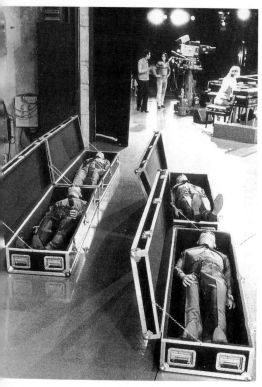

ぴあ

PNN NEWS

SCREEN
PLAY
MUSIC
NEW DISK
FM
ART
EVENT
LECTURE
BOOK

Above: Ralf Hütter in Florian Schneider's flat in Düsseldorf. (Martin Fraudreau)

Below: Ralf Hütter in the studio. (Martin Fraudreau)

Opposite Page.
Top: The group pose in front of their robot counterparts for the launch of *Man Machine* in Paris. Front row (l-r) Rupert Perry, Maxime Schmitt, Ralf Hütter, Karl Bartos, Wolfgang Flur and Florian Schneider. (Photo Jean-Luc Mabit)

Bottom left: The dummies "resting" before a TV performance in France. (Christian Rose)

Bottom right: Japanese magazine cover featuring the group. (Karl Bartos collection)

Top left: Florian Schneider on stage during the *Computer Word* tour. (François Branchon)

Below left: Ralf Hütter on stage during the *Computer World* tour. (François Branchon)

Top right: The group performing the popular "Pocket Calculator" part of their show. (François Branchon)

Below right: The inside of the Kling Klang studio in the early '80s. (Martin Fraudreau)

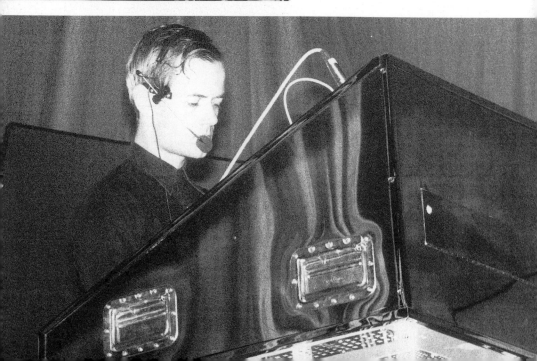

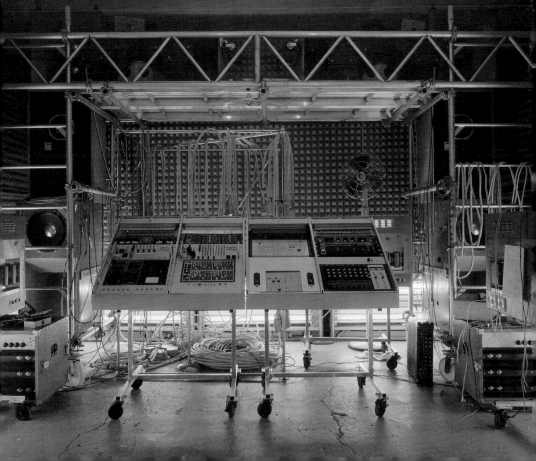

Above: One of the new style robots in action during the 1991 *The Mix* tour. (Aldo Soarez)

playing for hours and doodling around. Wolfgang looked after the design and stage set."[4]

Emil Schult confirms Schneider's unique input to the overall texture of the sound, as well as his role in pushing forward the group's application of technology:

"Florian was always the driving force, he was very inventive. When it came to making new developments, Florian was pushing things forward. He has a different speed of temperament. When it comes down to the extra embellishments to the music, that's Florian."[5]

In essence, although their music had vastly changed, their composing method hadn't actually altered that much over the years. Back in the early '70s Conny Plank had described the Kraftwerk working method as one of playing around until they hit upon something that they all liked. The only difference now was that the equipment that they were playing around with was more sophisticated. They were still composing by a process of improvisation and elimination. Maxime Schmitt:

"Often, they would all sit behind the console, letting the machines run by themselves for one or two hours, the sequencers, everything. From time to time Florian would stand up and go to another machine and start or launch another sequence. It was almost closer to a traditional jam session than to studio work. The following day they would listen back to the tape."[6]

From the long sections of recorded tape the group would sit down and criticise what they had produced, often for hours on end, finally deciding on the sections of music that they liked most. These sections were then refined and honed down to identifiable pieces or songs. The whole method of composing was one of a constant "work in progress", which could as much be applied to the group itself as it could the individual songs. Maxime Schmitt:

"It is close to the way of working on a film. Both in terms of the amount of material and the way of working. In fact, it's just like editing a film from all the rushes. Only when it's all edited you re-do the original. Because it was their studio, they didn't have to worry about time running out and they were able to work day after day. I was always worried that they might lose the essence and spontaneity of the original demo. But they didn't lose that soul. For me Kraftwerk has a soul, even though it was electronic and mathematic.

Ralf had notions of classical piano, so the melodies were classical. He would say, "Everything we are doing is classical, so our piece will be a classic". And I never saw the same strength in other groups. Chuck Berry had it, or people like that, but who after that had the strength to write classics? After, it was copies, like the Rolling Stones. Maybe The Who were more original. But the dynamic of a group, its classicism and its strength, was there in its entirety with Kraftwerk, and it was really given by Ralf."[7]

At that time, Hütter's view of the way Kraftwerk operated was the only one people had to go by, as he had been become the sole mouthpiece. Emil Schult:

"Ralf was like an unappointed leader, he was the spokesman. It was like a group where everyone had his positions. I was doing a lot of administrative and support work on the road. Everybody at this point was equally contributing to the growth of the group. Whilst commercially or financially, Ralf and Florian were leading, Karl and me were also participating."[8]

As Schult implies, musically the group were becoming well organised, like a company where everyone had their specific duties. In fact, in the studio each member now had his own workstation consisting of a bank of instruments on which they could improvise. But on a business level their affairs were much more confused. As Hütter explained to the journalist Sylvain Gire, "We are not a big company which is organised in a military way, we are very anarchic and very individualistic."[9]

This anarchic approach was enhanced by the fact that they stoically refused to take the obvious step of having a manager, even though this would have been justified by their increasing prominence. The reticence to place Kraftwerk's destiny in the hands of an outside party came from Hütter and Schneider, although it was clear that these matters had been discussed. Equally clearly it was something that the outwardly harmonious group disagreed about. As Schult says, "They always refused. My idea was to get a secretary to care for the fans etc, but it didn't go through, they didn't want it, so it didn't get done."[10]

In reality, Hütter was acting as the manager with help from Maxime Schmitt who advised on some of the day-to-day business affairs of being in a group. Kling Klang was nonetheless a fully registered publishing-production company by now, whose profits, like those of any other company, were mostly re-invested. Schmitt was involved in giving advice on which equipment to invest in, as he had worked with other bands in commercial studios. Also, in his capacity as EMI's principal contact with the group, he was ever mindful of the need for potential hit records. Maxime Schmitt:

> "I was thinking, "Is there a good song coming out of this?" or "will the stuff that I heard be as good in three months?" There was this quest where I wanted to bring back something really strong. I remember I used to go to Düsseldorf and I would listen to the new material, saying, "But there you are not doing Kraftwerk anymore, you are doing a sort of Queen!" And they would say, "After all, maybe it's not bad, maybe it can be a new direction." But in fact, they came back very fast to their style. When things went towards new directions, within six months it had become recognisably Kraftwerk again."[11]

However, Schmitt's advice aside, on most other matters Hütter increasingly acted as a kind of filter, whereby most offers, correspondence or whatever, were at best being ignored. Ultimately, as they were too wary of employing a manager, most of the career decisions were in his and Schneider's hands. Maxime Schmitt:

> "Even if there have been a number of musicians who are Kraftwerk, their thinking head has always been Ralf. It is difficult to explain, but it's obvious in a group you have to have a leader. Florian was very important in terms of the concept – he had excellent judgement because he had that distance to be objective about the music."[12]

Consistent with Schmitt's assessment of the hierachy that was operating, *Man Machine*'s concept and production was credited to Hütter and Schneider alone. However, the clearly defined musical delegation within the group resulted in their most discernably cohesive LP so far.

Man Machine sported one of the group's most startling covers. Reproduced totally in black and red, the cover artwork by Karl Klefisch was inspired by the Russian artist El Lissitzky. As such the typefaces and cubist shapes are clearly a tribute or homage to the Russian constructivist art of the early 1920s. Apparently the group were wary of plagiarizing Lissitzky too much, adding the phrase "inspired by El Lissitzky" on the cover, as the lawyer who looked after the artist's estate was based in Düsseldorf.

The front cover features a Günther Fröhling photograph of the group standing on a descending staircase dressed in red shirts and black ties – all the group having accentuated black eyebrows and bright red lips. In typically meticulous fashion, they spent a lot of time picking exactly the right stairs that would fit in with the Kraftwerk image. On the back cover, they are standing on the same stairs in the same attire with their heads at 90 degrees and their left hand on their hips. This picture, like the Bavarian scene on *Trans-Europe Express*, was not without a touch of irony if not camp humour.

In fact, *Man Machine*'s cover is full of contradictions. Clearly the image of a German group dressed in military-type uniforms could be conceived as controversial and having possible austere fascistic overtones (red & black being the Nazi colours). However, the ever dominant red, together with the fact that the group are facing East in both photographs make it clear that there was an Eastern European influence at work. In fact, Hütter actually speaks a bit of Russian and has family connections in former East Germany. All this, combined with the Russian influenced artwork, including the Russian subtitle, made the Communist implications prevalent. It was a brilliant juxtaposition of politically influenced images. As Karl Bartos remembers, *"Man Machine* had a strong paramilitary image, but it is a contradiction because we wore red shirts and not brown."[13]

Kraftwerk weren't alone in attracting controversy by using such apparently confrontational tactics. In the art world, both Anselm Kiefer and Gilbert & George had achieved considerable notoriety by utilising elements of fascist imagery. A lot of people saw the irony of such artistic statements, but inevitably some took it at face value and wrongly assumed it was endorsing fascism.

Ironically, *Man Machine*, provisionally entitled "Dynamo", saw the group moving away from specifically Germanic references. (It is possible that the title "Dynamo" was dropped due to its footballing connotations.) In the end, the LP was subtitled in three languages – the German version in English, French and Russian (even though there were no French or Russian versions of the LP). Putting interpretations of the cover aside, they were beginning to create a feeling of universality about their music that transcended political, cultural or even language barriers. Even more than that, by adopting a uniform they were stressing the corporate mentality of the group as one whole, Kraftwerk being greater than the sum of its parts. An efficient working machine whose individual personalities had given way to a group mentality.

Even on first listening it was clear that *Man Machine* had a much lighter feel than its predecessor, the electronic percussion being simpler, more subtle and less intrusive. The LP has "classic" stamped all over it, and as a standard of its type, it is evocative of a certain period. In time it would acquire the same ageless quality as The Beatles' *Sergeant Pepper* or The Beach Boys' *Pet Sounds* without ever achieving anyway near the same in terms of sales. This "classic" quality was attained by simplifying the music even further than *Trans-Europe Express*. The combination of electronic rhythms and precise melodies perfectly symbolised the group's approach to the clean efficiency of their sound. Despite the technically perfect way the album was put together, it was far from clinical. So much so that for the first time it was possible to speak about about an "electronic sensuality", or of the "warmth of machines". Consistent with the LP's title, Kraftwerk had now perfected the synthesis of injecting a human personality into their equipment and extracting a mechanical sensibility in return. Bono from U2 recently told the *NME* that Kraftwerk are "one of the modern soul statements." [14] Ralf Hütter:

"The dynamism of the machines, the "soul" of the machines, has always been a part of our music. Trance always belongs to repetition, and everybody is looking for trance in life etc., in sex, in the emotional, in pleasure, in anything, in parties, in... So, the machines produce an absolutely perfect trance." [15]

All six tracks on *Man Machine* have the same homogenous feel, with more or less the same texture, that of synthesizers, rhythm boxes and vocoded voices. With the exception of the criminally catchy "The Model" all the pieces are about the same length with no obvious pivotal or central track. Each has its own very crafted feel, giving the impression that as much attention has been paid to what has been left out as to what has been put in. The electronic gadgetry of the past seems to have totally disappeared. Each song is now like a piece of hi-tech machinery that has been developed, tested and manufactured or "machined" in a very conscientious way.

Like *Trans Europe Express*, the LP could be loosely described as another concept album, dealing with themes of the future – robots and space travel amongst other things. But the overall theme of the LP is really summed up in the title, being a celebration of the connection between humans and technology, or an idealised type of marriage between man and machine. Strictly speaking, rather than the LP being a concept, the group themselves were now the concept, and the LP was merely a vehicle to further it. Again similarities might be drawn with Warhol, whose personality came to embody the central conceptual focus of his art, his later paintings merely embellishing the Warhol persona.

The LP opens with "The Robots" which developed the idea of "Showroom Dummies" from their previous LP and also extended the cover concept of the group as one integral whole – one machine. This effectively brought together their sound and image as one. More than any other track it has become a trademark with its lyric which states that "we are the robots" – a precursor to the idea that they would later use of actually recreating the image of themselves in the form of robots. Also, with the line "dancing mekanik" they were hinting that one day the robots themselves would actually move or dance.

The mostly instrumental "Spacelab" clearly reflects a time when spaceflight was having to be curtailed due to economic reasons. As a result the Americans and Russians had turned their attention away from the "man on the moon" exploits of the late '60s and more toward the assembling of laboratories in space. Despite their interest in modern technology, this is the only time that Kraftwerk would turn their attention toward space, generally preferring more earthly concerns. The side finishes with "Metropolis" which is clearly a reference to the Fritz Lang cult film of the same name, and Hütter still acknowledges the influence of such old film makers. By setting an old film title within an album dedicated to futurist concerns, they had once again pulled their old trick of juxtaposing old and new imagery, this time within one song.

Side two opens with "The Model", which clocks in at a modest 3 minutes 39 seconds, and on the face of it is a self-explanatory tale of a model in a magazine. However, it is fairly unique in that it is the only Kraftwerk song to have any specific female references. The group felt that the rather robotic posture of catwalk models was in keeping with the group's image. It is also the only track which really jumps out of the album's futurist concept and is the only visible indication that Emil Schult was still involved with the group, as he is credited with co-writing the lyric. "The Model" is the archetype of a high quality electro-pop dance track with its eminently whistleable tune and was the obvious choice for a single. Being their most accessible song it has been covered by other artists on a number of occasions, the most notable versions being by long-time Resident's collaborator Snakefinger (Philip Lithman), and the Japanese band Hikashu. More recently in 1986 Big Black recorded a rock version of the song on their *Songs About Fucking* LP. Also, the French female singer Robert has recorded a version in German.

"Neon Lights" is probably the most complex track on the LP, building in synthesized layers and conjuring up a city waking up bathed in neon light – a sublimely atmospheric piece. Finally comes the title track which rather laboriously trails through the words 'Man Machine' sung in vocoded arpeggios, providing the LP with the now familiar repetitive coda.

The *Man Machine* LP was launched in Paris, with a press party at the top of the newly built Tour Montparnasse – the invitations stressing that everyone was to wear red. When people arrived the newly created dummies of the group were on display dressed in their red shirts and black ties and the album was played to the expectant throng.

The idea of creating dummies of the group had come from a number of disparate sources. The dummies obviously represented an extension of the inanimate posing that the group had adopted for previous publicity photographs. However, the initial idea had come about on an earlier lengthy tour of America, when they began to feel that the arduous nature of the tour was turning them into robots or dummies. They were also intrigued by the coincidence that the Russian word Robotnic meant 'worker'. At first the group had hit upon the idea of producing some kind of electronic dance/ballet, that they themselves would perform to convey this idea. This was eventually abandoned, probably as being too extrovert, in favour of the more starkly effective dummies which had been made by a Munich artist who had modified them from the bodies of actual showroom dummies.

At the launch for *Man Machine* the dummies did most of the promotion work, Kraftwerk themselves remaining hidden from the press for all but five minutes, when they put in an appearance dressed all in black with red ties (the opposite of the LP sleeve). Some people marvelled at this as a statement of minimalism, but some of the press felt they had been snubbed by the group, writing pieces which chastised by saying things like, "the Germans who don't even say Good Evening." However, there were enough souvenir grabbers present for the dummies to be left nearly naked when the evening had finished.

Shortly after the Paris launch party, Maxime Schmitt arranged for the group to appear on a new French TV programme. This was one of the few public appearances Kraftwerk actually made wearing their *Man Machine* uniforms. Maxime Schmitt:

> "I was at the George V Hotel with the boss of Capitol records. I was excited because it was through my job that I had managed to get Kraftwerk on TV in France on a Sunday! When he saw the broadcast, he jumped back saying, "who signed that!?" I explained that Rupert Perry (head of A&R) had signed them, and his response was, "Why has Rupert signed such a thing, I must speak with him!"[16]

On the whole, there was a hostile reaction to the group's adoption of their red-shirted starkly paramilitary image, and *Man Machine*'s cover was initially rejected in the States possibly due to its communist implications. It may well have been as a result of this adverse reaction that there was no accompanying tour. "Spacelab" was never adopted into their live repertoire, "Metropolis" only played once or twice, whilst "Neon Lights" was featured on the later 1981 tour but not subsequently. Both "The Model" and "The Robots" are still featured regularly in live sets today. However, Karl Bartos feels that there were also other reasons for the lack of a tour at the time:

"They didn't like to tour, especially Florian. You get up in the morning, 7 or 8 o'clock you go to the airport, or to the bus, you travel for hours, you arrive, you go to the hotel, you go to the concert hall, the concert lasts for one and a half hours and the rest is full of shit. Because of all the travelling you are tired all the time."[17]

There were, of course, plenty of offers from promoters wishing to stage concerts by the group. Maxime Schmitt:

"That's one of my biggest regrets, that there was never a tour based around the red shirts and the *Man Machine* concept. They received fantastic offers to play, like New Year's Eve at *Le Palace* (the most exclusive club in Paris at the time), but they did not want to do it.

This was exactly at the time when there was a huge demand for the group, a tour could have seen a great explosion of interest in them. Particularly in America, where it would have helped to explain what Kraftwerk was all about. The Americans would have totally flipped seeing four guys with the red shirts and everything. Later in America, they came to appreciate the dance side of their music, but not the aesthetic, not this European side of the four guys in red."[18]

Despite there being no tour to promote *Man Machine*, the reaction from the public and critics alike to the LP was very favourable. It reached No 9 in the UK album charts selling more than 100,000 copies, whilst in France it clocked up sales of over 200,000 copies. In France, Schmitt had organised a large fly-posting campaign to coincide with the LP's release, so all over Paris there were the distinctive faces from the *Man Machine* cover staring at passers by. The group also reflected current trends by having various limited editions available in coloured vinyl, not to mention releasing a number of different singles which also featured tracks from previous LPs. The LP was available in Germany and France in a limited edition red vinyl, whilst "Neon Lights" was released as a 7" and 12" single on luminous vinyl together with "Trans-Europe Express" and "The Model".

Man Machine heralded the group having truly metamorphasized into the modern incarnation that they have continued to develop to the present day. This LP more than any other represented Kraftwerk's "Weltanschauung" (vision of the world). The music seems somehow ageless, presenting the musicians as sound engineers working in perfect symbiosis with their machines for the entertainment of the masses. It is one of the fundamental LPs of the 1970s, redefining people's appreciation of the link between technology and music, becoming hugely influential on other musicians.

The music press too, were beginning to acknowledge Kraftwerk's influence, and in 1978 the group rather belatedly made their first appearance on the front cover of the *NME*. Kraftwerk have always maintained an almost non-existent relationship with the press, despite generally favourable reviews. However, in a typical display of reticence, Kraftwerk failed to arrange for an original photograph to be used for the cover feature, and the paper had to be satisfied with a mere reproduction of the inside sleeve of *Man Machine*. This may go part of the way to explaining why to date this has remained one of the only front covers the group has achieved in the mainstream UK music press.

Very soon, it was clear that *Man Machine* was making a huge impact on many groups who were beginning to re-assess the contribution that synthesizers could make to pop music. It is not surprising that these new groups rejected the quasi-classical tinkerings of most of the synthesizer players of the past and looked to Kraftwerk as role models. The so-called "synthesizer boom" had been triggered by advances in instrument technology, particularly the production of cheap, portable keyboards and drum machines. This meant that those . on a limited budget could have similar access to the sounds and technology that Kraftwerk had. By the linking of drum machines to synthesizers via sequencers, new groups sprung up with the synthesizer as the central focus.

So, as a reaction to the largely guitar-based punk movement, a whole new generation of keyboard orientated groups started coming out of Britain. Ultravox, The Human League, Orchestral Manouvres In The Dark, Soft Cell, Depeche Mode all became linked with a movement that laboured under the rather foppish tag of the 'New Romantics'. Whilst the punk groups had looked toward the US guitar based bands like The Stooges for inspiration, the New Romantic groups were much more European in outlook, and with their flailing fringes, make-up, androgenous looks and tinkling synthesizers, they were obviously more influenced by Bowie, Roxy Music and principally Kraftwerk.

So, whilst the early Depeche Mode adopted Kraftwerk's stage presence of four keyboard operators stood in a line, Gary Numan donned a black shirt and tie, and produced one of the biggest hits of 1979 in "Our Friends Electric". Similarly, The Human League came up with the idea of sending tape players and slide projectors as the support slot to a Talking Heads tour of the UK, while the group stayed at home. This was an idea almost certainly stolen from Kraftwerk (or at very least influenced by their earlier taped support slot for Bowie). The tour promoter was none too keen about this idea and promptly threw The Human League off the tour.

Hits followed for many of the New Romantic groups, many of whom did little to hide the debt that they owed to their German mentors. By accident or design OMD even named one of their LPs *Organisation*. They also more recently covered "Neon Lights" on their 1991 LP *Sugar Tax*. This rather poor cover version only went to highlight how sadly lacking in staying power and inspiration many of the British "synthesizer boom" bands were later to become. In fact, it wasn't long before most of these bands had partially forsaken synthesized music and returned to more conventional instruments.

However, just as Kraftwerk were reaching their peak in terms of influence in the 1970's, they entered the first of many periods of extended silence that would continue to punctuate their career to the present day. Following 1978's *Man Machine*, no more records would appear by the group for a further three years until 1981. They were no doubt conscious that leaps forward in technology meant the competition had in some ways caught up with them. A situation that found the group pleased by the attention but slightly less than flattered by the imitation. Karl Bartos:

"We had a lot of different reactions all at the same time. I would say it's always good to have competition, even if you just have a shop in the street. It makes you stronger in some ways because you have to look around and listen to what they are doing, what is their approach to it. But there was never really anybody who had that strong a connection with us. There has always been that silly English pop scene, with silly lyrics."[19]

So, for the most part, the hiatus that was the New Romantic period passed without any direct new contribution from Kraftwerk themselves, with the exception of being constantly on the turntables of Steve Strange and Rusty Egan's London clubs that were at the centre of the movement. Despite being largely responsible for it, Kraftwerk wisely avoided involving themselves with the British synthesizer boom. Having previously managed to shake off the "Kraut Rock" tag, they weren't going to suddenly ally themselves with any new musical movement or trend. Their refusal to endorse the advent of synthesizer pop was especially wise. The instrument was by now an affordable and widely available item, and as a result its fortunes tended to waver nearly as hysterically as some of the efforts of those who tried to play them. Kraftwerk, as ever, remained largely uncommunicative, elusive and hidden within the fortress-like walls of the Kling Klang studio as if waiting for the storm to blow over.

CALCULATORS
and
DISCOS

THE *COMPUTER WORLD* LP RELEASED BY EMI IN MAY OF 1981 WAS initially viewed by some as cynically oversimplistic. On reflection, many found it was arguably Kraftwerk's most cohesive and conceptual piece of work yet. The LP was conceived at Kling Klang between 1978 and 1981 – a length of time that reflected the group's increasingly slow and arduous working method. However, it was inconceivable that the LP actually took three years to record, much of the gap being explained by the fact that the studio had now been modified so that all the equipment could be taken out on tour. This meant that the studio layout and the stage set were now to all intents and purposes identical, much of the equipment being rebuilt to alleviate the problems of transportation and hours of messy rewiring that had accompanied previous live performances. As Hütter put it, "Our studio is our electronic living room, our little house, so we take it with us."[1]

The tone of *Computer World* is set by the title track, and it wasn't exactly difficult to reach the conclusion that the LP was essentially one which acknowledged that the world was now heavily reliant on computer technology of one sort or another. As the EMI press release stated, "The concept of the album is that this *is* the Computer World. Every facet of our society is now influenced by computer technology, and our language has become the language of computer software."[2] Or as Hütter put it even more succinctly, "We live in a computerworld, so we are making a song about it."[3]

So, unlike *Man Machine*, which looked at the larger concerns of technology such as space labs, *Computer World* addressed the everyday concerns of micro-computer technology and miniaturisation that were now affecting the home, business and educational environments. Ralf Hütter:

> "We like to portray the things we do on a day-to-day basis in our music – other people might be fascinated by space flights to the moon and so on. We did try a space lab kind of set once, but always prefer now to relate to everyday technology, such as cars, trains and other human controlled machines."[4]

Compared with the previous couple of LPs, *Computer World* has a playful mood about it. The front cover, reproduced totally in yellow and black, features the heads of the four members recreated on a computer terminal. (Such have been the advances in computer technology that both the images on the screen and the keyboard already look dated by today's standards). On the back cover the four dummies stand at their consoles, seemingly poised and ready for action. The inner sleeve features the dummies in uniform, this time with their pocket hand-held devices. Hütter's dummy holds a mini keyboard whilst Schneider's holds a calculator, Bartos' dummy is seen playing a stylophone and Flur's is operating what looks like a radio controlled device of some sort. On the back of the inside sleeve the four dummies are once again photographed at their consoles, only this time from the back. Both the consoles and the hand-held devices had been designed and built by Wolfgang Flur in his own workshop. All the cover photos were taken inside the Kling Klang studio.

It was evident that Kraftwerk, or in all probability Hütter, had now hit upon the idea of letting the dummies take over the duty of being photographed for LP sleeves and promotional work. "We thought that photo-sessions wasted a lot of time, so they did a lot of them. At the same time we could get on with our studio plans"[5], Hütter informed *The Face*. This decision is one from which there seems to be no point of return. As a visual statement it was totally in keeping with their Man Machine concept, but it was also a neat way of sidestepping further publicity or promotional photos on which the group had never been keen. Within their ideal world, Hütter was already cherishing the future possibility of conceiving a robot programmed with a special memory or artificial intelligence which he could send in his place to be interviewed. Time will tell if this dream will be realised. Ralf Hütter:

> "You, the journalists, you will be amazed. One day, the robots will be the ones who will answer your questions, they will have an electronic brain and memories with all the possible questions. To get the answers, you will only have to press a button..."[6]

On the inner sleeve of *Computer World*, the four names of Hütter, Schneider, Flur and Bartos are lost amongst a host of other name credits. Nowhere does it mention who these people are and what their contribution to the LP is. Some names like Emil Schult and engineers Peter Bollig, Joachim Dehmann and Günther Spachtholtz are self-explanatory. Other people namechecked are Maxime Schmitt and Takeshi Shikura, their label managers in France and Japan respectively. Also credited is their New York lawyer Marvin Katz, along with Matten and Wiechers in Bonn where they bought much of their equipment. Various other contributors to artwork, DJs and promoters are also mentioned – all presumably considered by the group as important in some way and making up a sort of Kraftwerk "family".

Just as computers and global communication seemed to be making the world an ever smaller place, so *Computer World* reflected the group's continuing ambition of trying to create a universal music. While computer language itself was now a universal one which ignored linguistic differences, so the LP was an attempt to do the same. Although their music in the past had aquired an increasingly international flavour with tracks recorded in different languages, each of the previous LPs had retained some German connections. *Computer World* built upon *Man Machine*'s attempt to produce a type of global music.

Having said that, the title track "Computer World" which opens side one could be interpreted as having some specific German references. Although the track evokes the different international intelligence organisations like Interpol, the FBI and Scotland Yard, it was released at a time when terrorism had returned to the political stage. Germany was still reeling under the shock of the return of the Rote Armee

Fraktion (Red Army Faction). Just when their actions in the '70s had seemingly passed, they killed thirteen people in a terrorist attack in Münich on September 26th, 1980. "Computer World" also seemed to reflect the continuing concern about the use or misuse of computerised files of information in the hands of police authorities. In Germany in particular there was some concern and controversy about the famous central police file based in Wiesbaden.

Early on, the spoken lyric establishes a somewhat bleak warning about the dawning of a computerised world with its, "business, numbers, money, people". Later in the track this changes to the more human face of computerisation which was making "time, travel, communication, entertainment" all the easier.

In contrast, the following track, "Pocket Calculator", which was released as a single in 12" and cassette format just prior to the album, is light and playful. The track uses the sounds of Casio and Texas calculators and was recorded in a number of different languages – the German, French and English LPs all have their respective versions (certain sources also claim that there are Spanish and Polish versions which have never officially been released). As recognition of the influence that Japan was now having on the group, the B-side of the single is "Dentaku" which is the Japanese translation of the single's title and is sung in Japanese.

"Numbers" is a highly rhythmically based piece, which by its title is fairly self-explanatory. The exclusively vocoded vocal counts from one to eight in various different languages including English, German, Russian, Japanese, Spanish and French. Utilising these different languages in a very attractive and simplistic way was a means of emphasizing the group's new international agenda. The track also provided an ideal start for their live shows with its minimal vocal line serving as a kind of countdown to the beginning of their performances. "Numbers" runs directly into "Computer World 2" which is a reprise of the opening track, and indicates how future live shows would start with "Numbers" only to segue directly into "Computer World".

Side two opens with "Computer Love" which clearly extends the group's interest in the relationship between man and machine. But the track is also a kind of computerised blues with the lonely sounding

Hütter singing the lines, "I am alone, I don't know what to do, I need a rendezvous." Could this be the first robot blues?

"Home Computer", probably more than any other track, prophesies the rise of techno and house music in the '80s and '90s with its spacey sounding segments and syncopated electronic rhythm, over which the same two-line couplet is spoken at various intervals. It is no surprise that this was to become one of their most sampled pieces. In fact, the track itself indicates that Kraftwerk may have been doing some early sampling for themselves. The first five second burst of electronic bleeps bears a remarkable similarity with the musical motif of a Texas Instruments game entitled "Speak & Spell" which appeared on the market in 1980. This reference was not out of keeping with the Kraftwerk image. Maxime Schmitt:

"There is a something very child-like in Kraftwerk. It's this thing of "I play a little melody", it's always that. Ralf is a very complex person and his big strength is to write very simple melodies. Often, you find that the converse happens, that simple people write very complex things. With Kraftwerk, they are outstandingly intelligent, and possibly because of their German temperament, they cannot bear to do something complex.

I remember once when I was visiting Ralf at his home, he was playing on his white piano for his two year old niece. And this melody, I will always remember it, it pursued me for 5 or 6 years, and it never appeared on a record."[7]

The LP finishes with "It's More Fun To Compute" which musically is really just a continuation of "Home Computer". However, the title has a double-edged irony, again displaying Kraftwerk's tongue-in-cheek humour. Whilst it reflects the LP's concept of computerisation, it is also a joke play on words referring to the caption on a particular brand of pin-ball machine which states, 'It's more fun to compete', thus making the connection between computer games and a more old fashioned game. Again, the future and past mixed together.

Possibly spurred on by this irony, Neil Rowland in an interview in the *Melody Maker* in July 1981, asked Hütter what his opinion was of games like Space Invaders. Ralf Hütter:

"Yes, I find that very sad because you could play so many interesting games other than shooting, that shows again how sick they are, the only thing they think about is shooting each other. If they don't do it physically then they do it mentally on a screen."[8]

"It's More Fun To Compute" closes the album by providing the now familiar coda, bringing the LP full circle. Just like "Endless Endless" from *Trans-Europe Express* and "Man Machine" from the album of the same name, a very simple phrase is repeated over and over making the perfect closing for the LP.

In a pop music world becoming ever more susceptible to gimmickry, in some countries EMI accompanied review copies with a real pocket calculator with 'Kraftwerk – Computer World' printed in yellow and black at the top. This has inevitably become a much sought-after collector's item amongst the group's fans.

Promotional gimmicks aside, many critics went on to state that *Computer World* was their most finely tuned and considered LP. Certainly, every note and beat on the album seems to have been crafted to a minimalistic perfection, like a thoroughbred racing machine stripped down and streamlined to its barest component parts. This is an opinion that is shared by Karl Bartos, who considers it the best album the group has produced. Certainly, streamlined is an adequate way of describing its length, being a mere 16 minutes a side, but Kraftwerk as ever were living testimony that quantity doesn't necessarily equal quality.

However, lost on many was that the album was as much a warning about the dangers of a "computer world" as it was a celebration of the micro-technology that had brought computerisation into people's everyday lives. Many of the pieces were actually cautionary, concerning the loss of individualism that computerisation carried in its wake. Maxime Schmitt:

"It was a political album. Totally. The denunciation of the machines, the denunciation of the police and of the financial institutions as you can hear in the "Computer World" track. They are very... you cannot say socialist because the word doesn't mean anything anymore... but they have the intelligence to understand that in today's world you can't be an individual. There are so many people on Earth that inevitably you have to be socialist, in the purest sense of the word. And the album was a bit like that, it was going against the FBI, the Deutsche Bank, the machines, the computers, and the truth was coming in "Home Computer" and "Pocket Calculator"..."[9]

The album reached No 15 in the UK charts, and a number of singles were released from it. In the UK, "Computer Love" was released as the second single reaching No 36 in the charts. (Schmitt's suggestion that they record a French version with former model Carole Bouquet had been rejected by the group. His idea had been that the mannequin looking Bouquet, who was well known as a former James Bond girl from *For Your Eyes Only*, would appear almost like a female robot).

Strangely radio DJs concentrated more on the B-side of the single which was "The Model" from the previous LP. Subsequently, EMI remarketed the single with the sides reversed and it re-entered the charts becoming a top forty hit in Germany, and a number 1 hit in the UK in December 1981. Incidentally, when "The Model" was released in France, the group forced their record company to withdraw the sleeve as it featured the words "Number 1 in England" on it.

To date, "The Model" remains Kraftwerk's most successful record in the UK, helped by a video the group had made in conjunction with Hans-Otto Mertens. In this, they reverted to the tried and tested trick of using nostalgic imagery, this time from old German and French television news clips from the 50's and swinging 60's featuring notably Pierre Balmain and Yves Saint-Laurent models on the catwalk.

It is interesting that Kraftwerk's biggest single success should have been with a track which is perhaps one of the least synonymous with their image. Obviously the track crossed over and had a wider appeal than their traditionally rather male-orientated audience. Karl Bartos:

"I think if you take technique as the main subject for your output it is more attractive to boys. If you are Bryan Ferry and you talk about your feelings and how you are a jealous guy, then you reach the girls. Maybe with a song like "The Model" we had a crossover success."[10]

In reality, the success of "The Model" was probably just more evidence, if anyone needed it, that Kraftwerk were at least a couple of years (or a whole LP's worth) ahead of their time. This was further enhanced by the teen appeal of Depeche Mode and the Human League, showing that teenagers were finally ready to embrace synthesized pop music. Kraftwerk's record company attempted to cash in on the success of "The Model" with a flurry of re-issues which included the LP *Trans-Europe Express* and a single of "Showroom Dummies". (Two years later, in an attempt to repeat the experience of "The Model", EMI re-released "Computer Love" as a single in the UK – but the re-marketing trick didn't work as well the second time around).

With such a critically acclaimed and mesmerically catchy LP as *Computer World* under their belts, and with a studio now modified to be taken on tour, it was not surprising that the group undertook their most extensive tour yet. In fact, it was the group's first, and to date only world tour, taking in many of the capitals of what Hütter now liked to refer to as the "global village". Karl Bartos:

> "There were a lot more concerts in the '70s, afterwards not so many. Although the *Computer World* tour was maybe the longest, sixty dates around the world including Australia, Eastern Europe and Japan. My strongest impressions are of the concerts in Japan, because Japan was always a big influence on us. And Poland, it was amazing to play there. We played a lot in America also, once [*Autobahn* tour] we stayed there for ten weeks."[11]

The tour, consisting of around 90 dates in six months, demonstrated that the last three years had not been idled away. Starting off in Florence in May they unveiled much of their new streamlined electronic hardware. Schneider, for instance, now had a custom built flute synthesizer which he had designed and made himself. This was a synthesizer whose notes were triggered by the holes on the flute, thus allowing Schneider to play the tunes as if they were on a traditional flute.

The group also took with them four large video screens that had been made specially by Sony in Japan. Much of the intervening time between tours had been taken up compiling the video and film footage for these screens and working on the problem of how to synchronise this important visual input with the music. A successful example of this was the video for "Trans-Europe Express" where train carriage buffers coupled together in time with the rhythm of the music. As

Hütter himself put it, "Video can say more. During the concerts, we want the videos we show to enlarge our music, increase its prophetic and visionary side."[12]

For the stage set, each member of the group stood as before in a semi-circle with a console in front of them and the new video screens behind. The films were all synchronised over the four screens, each screen showing an identical image. This provided a more uniform identity to the visuals, and in typical minimalist fashion avoided diluting the effect by putting different images over the four screens. In front of them were the now familiar fluorescent name boxes reflecting the fixed stage placing of (left to right) Ralf, Karl, Wolfgang, Florian. The idea of the semi-circle was once again to portray the symmetry of the group as a working machine where no one person or element dominated. This was further enhanced by the tour uniform of black trousers and black shirts that the group had now adopted – a modification from the days of the shirts and ties of the *Man Machine* LP cover and launch. By losing the ties and the brightness of the red, and concentrating on the more neutral black, they no longer looked quite so paramilitary.

For the tour they were accompanied by Gunther Spachtholz as visual and lighting engineer, and sound engineer Joachim Dehmann who handled the final balance of the output from each member of the group, at any time mixing up to eight different sound sources. They also used sheet music and graphic diagrams in front of them detailing when to switch on or off certain sounds as well as reminders of certain of the harmony lines. They were also assisted by three other technicians as well as Emil Schult who was described by the group as being "the vibrations manager".

The concerts were preceded by 30 minutes or so of mood setting soft electronic noises as people entered the hall. The audience was then greeted by the robot voice saying, "Meine Damen und Herren, Ladies and Gentlemen, heute abend aus Deutschland, die Mensch-Machine – KRRRAFT–WERRRK". The two hour set featured; "Numbers", "Computer World", "Computer Love" and "Home Computer" from their new LP; "The Model", "The Robots", "Neon Lights" from *Man Machine*; "Hall of Mirrors", "Showroom Dummies" and "Trans-Europe Express" from the LP of the same name;

"Radio-Activity", "Ohm Sweet Ohm" and "The Voice of Energy" from *Radio-Activity* and inevitably "Autobahn". For the encore they returned to their new LP playing "Pocket Calculator" and "It's More Fun To Compute".

Although stressing the increased flexibility of their new equipment, the set was remarkably consistent in its running order, suggesting either that the group did not wish to fluctuate in this respect, or that the complex technology now dictated that this had to be the case. For a group who had started as being one of the early pioneers of a new improvised music, by 1981 their live performances had become as clearly and strictly regimented as their electronic lifestyle.

The *Computer World* tour which finished in Utrecht in December was an unqualified success covering Southern Europe, Germany, Britain, France, East Germany, Poland, Australia, India, Japan and America. The group were intrigued by the reaction to their music in Japan and particularly India, where they wondered what sort of response they would get to their hi-tech show in such strange surroundings as Bombay. In the more familiar territory of America, with a typical piece of Kraftwerk humour, they delighted in telling journalists that they carried around small scissors to snip the offending wires in elevators which provided Muzak – which the group referred to as "sound pollution".

The tour proved that the total mobility of the studio was a realisable goal. The perfect synthesis of man and machine working in harmony to create a piece of technical entertainment that, considering its potential, was breathtaking in its economy of image and sound. Was this a studio band playing live, or a live band playing the studio? Kraftwerk had once again neatly sidestepped the temptation to produce an overblown multi-media extravaganza, similar to those like Pink Floyd's *The Wall*. Instead of building their equipment up around like some kind of technological ego trip, they saw themselves as presenting a more low profile image. As Hütter put it, "bringing man and machine together in a friendly partnership of musical creation."[13]

For their efforts, the group now found that rather than standing and staring, audiences were beginning to dance at their concerts, a development that clearly pleased them as they were becoming constant and enthusiastic visitors to discotheques as part of their daily routine. Ralf Hütter:

> "We have always played in different situations, in different countries, different cultures. And, of course, when we were playing for example in America, there was always a large part of the audience which was dancing, the black audience, hispanic, hispano-American, etc.... Electronic music is really a world language, it is the music of the global village."[14]

In general, the group themselves moved little on stage, apparently in an attempt to emphasize the robotic aspect of their music, but also probably out of a sense of awkwardness with their role as entertainers. However, it was clear that they were enjoying themselves, and Hütter's vocals in particular were generally more relaxed, even crooning the catchy tunes to "The Model" and "Computer Love". They also featured a new middle section to "Autobahn", which included the lines in German, "Always again on the autobahn" and "Every day for four hours on the autobahn", as well as listing imaginary journeys like, "From Zurich to Brussels, from Brussels to Hamburg". "Hall of Mirrors" differed markedly from the LP version having much more of an electric piano sound to it. In Utrecht, they even played an upbeat version of "Metropolis", but this was not a common feature of the tour.

The group made little attempt to communicate directly with their audience, the exception being during the encore "Pocket Calculator" where members of the audience were invited to play the little hand held devices created for the song. The devices were actually modified from instruments they had found in a department store the previous Christmas. These were then connected by cables to the main consoles. In interviews Hütter delighted in explaining how this could have been achieved by use of radio control instead of a cable, but that they had forsaken that idea as the cable gave them the feeling of being linked like robots to their main control machine. He also stressed how these gadgets continued to show how the group utilised everyday items from "street level" and incorporated them into their musical arsenal.

The tour also unveiled for the general public the dummies/robots who at the end of the set appeared alongside the group on stage during "The Robots". The dummies were similar, if not identical to those that had been previewed to the press at the launch of *Man Machine* some three years earlier and the same as those on the *Computer World* sleeve. Rumour has it that the dummies even sat in the audience for part of the show on selected dates, but Kraftwerk were rather dismayed when they discovered that they had to pay for their seats!

Schult, who accompanied the group on most of the *Computer World* tour, had begun to have some misgivings about the direction in which the group was heading, especially regarding the concept of the robots. Emil Schult:

> "My concept was to go more global, and to start co-operating with other artists. Especially when the robots started, the communication with other artists was forbidden, everything was exclusive to Kraftwerk, and it was too hard for me to live with this. And that was the reason why the last tour I participated in was in 1981."[15]

Schult's description of communication being forbidden gives the impression that the group were indeed becoming almost obsessively secretive – perhaps even hiding behind their robot counterparts. Certainly, by the time of the *Computer World* tour, Hütter who was then 34, seemed more ill at ease about giving interviews. Whereas his early answers expounded the group's conceptual theories, he was now altogether more reserved and reflective.

However, the rest of the group had no objection to Hütter's central position as spokesman. It was generally accepted that Hütter, who other than his native German, speaks good English, French and Spanish, was the natural person to undertake these duties. Anyway, as he was the main instigator of the group's image, it was obvious that he was the best person for the job. Despite being slightly less talkative, he was likely to stress the central link between man and machine – but managing to retain more than a hint of humour. However, to the uninitiated it was sometimes difficult to differentiate which ideas were humorous caricatures, and which were indeed serious proposals for the future course of the group.

Through the '80s Hütter and Schneider became more publicity shy than ever and there was less and less dialogue between the group and the press. Rather than conducting formal interviews, they preferred to offer a few select journalists the opportunity to go to Düsseldorf, where they would create the appropriate atmosphere for the meeting or interview. Photographer Martin Fraudreau remembers one such occasion:

> "We were there for just one day. During the evening Ralf and Florian took us for a long drive around Düsseldorf in a large black Mercedes. We went by the steelworks, factories and industries – I wish I could have filmed that. I remember both of them were very intelligent and very polite."[16]

He was accompanied by Patrick Zerbib who described the experience in an article in *Actuel* magazine:

> "Düsseldorf, 11 pm. In Ralf's Mercedes, we speed our way to the Düsseltal, the industrial zone. When he wants to relax, Ralf drives for a good hour on these roads where nature and factories alternate. He drives at a constant speed, his two black gloves laid on the steering wheel, his face impassive like that of Doctor Mabuse. Suddenly, his features stiffen, he leans forward, the nape of his neck tensed. The car glides down a deserted road and Ralf shouts "Kraftwerk!".
>
> We have just passed the kraftwerk which gave its name to the group. It is the power station which gives Düsseldorf its electrical power. It appears on our left like a mountain of lights flickering, winking and flashing. Ralf was waiting for this moment to slip into the stereo a cassette of the next album."[17]

By the end of 1981, although they never boasted about such things, Kraftwerk were at the front of a technical revolution in home recording. They had prophesied much of the onslaught of a more accessible music technology, which Hütter had predicted would, "help to liberate people's creativity, allowing individuals to use the studio technology in their home for almost any sound they want."[18] In essence exactly what they had started out trying to achieve in their own "home studio" some ten years earlier. In March 1982, Hütter even supplied *Elecronics & Music Maker* and *The Face* magazines with the sheet music to the track "Computer World", so that their readers could reproduce the song at home on a casio or other synthesizer. This gesture seemed to be an electronic equivalent of the punk group's three chord philosophy of, "it's easy, anyone can do it".

Following the *Computer World* LP and tour, the group took what appeared to be one of their regular breaks from the limelight. They sat back and let others contemplate the technological vision that they had laid out before them. So, by 1982 Kraftwerk were not only an influence on the host of New Romantic synth-revellers who were now hugely popular in their own right, but more importantly their influence was stretching further afield. Synthesizers, drum machines and sequencers were now being adopted wholesale in black American dance music.

Probably the single most important factor in Kraftwerk's durability through the '80s in the face of their own declining output, was a record that came out of the burgeoning hip-hop scene of the Bronx in New York. Afrika Bambaataa and the Soul Sonic Force cut a record called "Planet Rock" that used the drum pattern from "Numbers" and the tune from "Trans Europe Express" as its central themes. This was at a time when sampling – the borrowing of melodies, phrases or snippetts of tunes from other records – was in its infancy. "Planet Rock", released in April 1982, went on to become a huge club hit worldwide, suddenly propelling the name of Kraftwerk back into the limelight and placing them at the centre of a whole new musical world.

The "Planet Rock" record was produced by Arthur Baker, who had been responsible for introducing Bambaataa to the music of Kraftwerk. Arthur Baker was a white producer/mixer, who together with John Robie, had become well accepted in the community of black musicians in New York. He helped create "electro" music, based around the Tommy Boy label, which had been started by Tom Silverman in 1981. "Electro" in itself was a natural extension of the rap movement which had begun around 1979/80 with Grandmaster Flash and Kurtis Blow.

Baker and other electro musicians fused elements of rap with European electronic music, borrowing influences from the British synthesizer boom with groups like the Human League, Yazoo, Gary Numan, Thomas Dolby and inevitably – Kraftwerk. Much of the awareness of these synthesizer groups in New York had been aided by Frankie Crocker on WBLS, whose station had switched from rock to disco in 1978, but who still chose to play groups like Kraftwerk. Being a fan of black music and European electronic music, Baker was the perfect person to mix the technologically obsessed world of Kraftwerk with the hip-hop movement. Arthur Baker:

"I always loved Kraftwerk, since the *Autobahn* LP which I had bought in Boston. At high school, I had begun to listen to rock music but also Philly soul. My hippy friends couldn't understand why I had records by Al Green and The Jackson Five in my bedroom! After that I got into Bowie's *Ziggy Stardust* and *Hunky Dory*. It was when I became a DJ that I discovered Kraftwerk, because it was possible to dance to it. Bambaataa loved that too: it was the quest for the perfect beat."[19]

In interviews around the time, Bambaataa also quoted Kraftwerk, Gary Numan and the Yellow Magic Orchestra as main influences in the electronic field. This interest in Kraftwerk from the black hip-hop scene did much to revive their flagging career in the US, which had waned after the initial success of *Autobahn*. However, whilst in New York to mix some tracks for the *Computer World* LP with François Kevorkian, Hütter and Schneider discovered for themselves that some of the people that had remained most faithful to Kraftwerk were the black DJs.

As a result, and most probably at Kevorkian's instigation, Hütter and Schneider visited clubs where hip-hop and Puerto Rican music was played. These were quite often gay or S&M clubs like The Loft and The Roxy. In these clubs, DJs were experimenting with mixing types of music together and making their own bootleg 12"s. One notable 12" was based on a tape loop of "Metal on Metal" from *Trans-Europe Express* and this was probably what prompted Arthur Baker and Afrika Bambaataa to use the title track as the basis of "Planet Rock".

François Kevorkian was a native of France who had fled to New York to avoid national service. Prior to his move, he had briefly played drums for the French group Magma. Kevorkian started by working as a DJ in various discotheques in Manhattan at night, and sleeping in a sleeping bag on the floor of the discos by day. He soon built up a reputation as being one of the first DJs to play around with cutting and splicing different tracks together. Soon, these hybrid "re-mixes" were being played on black radio stations all over New York. As Bartos recalls, "we bought maybe 20 or 30 records, and his name always seemed to be on the best of them, so we called him up."[20] Soon the group had rather affectionately nicknamed him "le croissant" and were working with him at the mixing desk at the aptly named Power Station studios in New York.

At this time the whole hip-hop movement had yet to explode into the mainstream, and the scene was very underground. On visiting New York it must have been a culture shock for Kraftwerk to be taken by Kevorkian to these clubs, which were often in fairly violent and dangerous areas where whites would rarely go. Many were essentially Puerto Rican and much of the latin hip-hop came to be based around the syncopated drum machine beat of claves. They incorporated rhythms from Cuba, Salsa and from the Antilles, but were also fascinated by the way Kraftwerk had fashioned a totally electronic sound.

As a result the club DJs, themselves highly competitive, were flattered to know that Kraftwerk were in town and checking out what was then a very new and exciting scene. After all, this was a time when many of the other synthesizer groups were saying that disco music sucked. Hütter and Schneider on the other hand were lucky enough to witness a new vibrant form of dance music at its birth.

So, just as Kraftwerk were an enormous influence on these DJs, so the club dance music of the early '80s in its turn influenced them. It is noticeable that from this period onwards they became increasingly aware of the black music scene, and as a result their own music grew to have a distinctly more danceable or club-wise edge. In fact, Hütter once told his friend Boris Venzen, "Our music is good if blacks and whites can dance to it at the same time."[21]

As the hip-hop scene progressed, so it spread to other cities in the US, each producing its own hybrid dance music. In Detroit, the home of Tamla Motown, producers like Derek May were fascinated by Kraftwerk and Depeche Mode. May, who was one of the founders of the techno scene in Detroit, said that some of the things that had driven him crazy when he was young, were European groups like Kraftwerk and underground dance records like "Los Ninos Del Parque" by the French/German cult group Les Liaisons Dangereuses, and even obscure instrumental pieces by the French group Martin Circus.

It was inevitable that as hip-hop and techno became increasingly popular, so the practice of sampling would become fraught with legal complications. The subsequent copyright wranglings surrounding the type of "sampling" on hip hop and techno records has been the source of much controversy in the music business. Although fascinated with the possibilities of sampling, Kraftwerk were understandably upset that their track had been so blatantly used without any acknowledgement of the original. Karl Bartos:

"With "Planet Rock", in the beginning we were very angry, because they didn't credit the authors. It was completely the melody off "Trans-Europe Express" and the rhythm track from "Numbers". So we felt pissed off. If you read a book and you copy something out of it, you do it like a scientist, you have to quote where you took it from, what is the source of it. And there was nothing written down saying that its source was "Trans-Europe Express" and "Numbers".[22]

Eventually Afrika Bambaataa's "borrowing" of the riff was the subject of a legal case that saw Kraftwerk apparently receive royalties from the track which has been subsequently re-titled "Planet Rock/Trans-Europe Express". Maxime Schmitt:

"He knew perfectly what he was using, he had not put the names of the authors and had not declared anything. Maybe he was thinking, "Oh, they are German, they will never follow it up."..."[23]

To list the number of samples that have been taken from Kraftwerk records would be an arduous and difficult task, but suffice to say that after James Brown they are probably the most sampled group of all. Recent records by Trouble Funk, Digital Underground, Cookie Crew, Doug Lazy, Kiss AMC, LFO, The Fearless Four, Eskimos and Egypt and Borghesia have all featured Kraftwerk samples to name just a few. The rhythms that have been sampled the most often are "The Robots", "The Model", "Numbers" and "Home Computer". However, Hütter is still characteristically cagey when asked about his position toward sampling:

"It depends. If it is a deejay record, a special record, a small bit... If it is a long bit, it's copyright. If someone takes a special sound, there's the copyright, and the publishing company have to deal with it."[24]

From the number of samples of Kraftwerk records, it is evident that their mastery of creating sounds and noises electronically was being recognised, particularly by those familiar with the recording process. Although, how they achieved these sounds is something the group refuses to talk about, remaining a closely guarded secret. Maxime Schmitt:

> "When we met people, the first question was, "Oh, how do you do your drums?" But it couldn't be explained, because Kraftwerk didn't use that sort of studio language."[25]

Ironically, in the end it was technology itself that gave others access to the exclusivity of Kraftwerk's music and the sounds they had given birth to. Rather than trying to copy or recreate certain groups' unique sound, many studios just equipped themselves with samplers and built up electronic libraries of these sounds. As a result, borrowed drum sounds from Kraftwerk or Led Zeppelin's John Bonham now appeared on all manner of records. Patrick Codenys from Front 242:

> "It's possible to identify some of them immediately, they are so personal. I've been to some studios in the USA, where there are these kinds of sound banks. Once, I think I saw a Front 242 CD. But in every studio they have the complete Kraftwerk CD collection!"[26]

With their music being acknowledged by two totally distinct sources, the electro-pop of the English groups and the hip-hop scene in the States, it was now impossible to ignore their influence, whether or not you agreed with their quasi-robotic posturing. Once again the name of Kraftwerk was a fashionable one to drop into conversation, and throughout the eighties their notoriety grew in remarkable leaps inversely proportional to their output. Their avant-garde beginnings were now a forgotten anecdote – the strange paradox was that four reclusive middle-aged Germans with suits and ties were increasingly at the centre of what was being perceived as extremely hip and trendy.

RHYTHMS
and
CYCLES

AS THE 1980s PROGRESSED, MANY STRUGGLED TO FIND OUT MORE about the mysterious group from Düsseldorf who had set the wheels of electronic pop and electronic dance music in motion. However, the group, or more specifically Hütter, had become increasingly wary of interviews and exposure. This may well be partly due to the fact that the group themselves were now fully aware of the reverence in which they were now being held and were reluctant to do anything to upset this. Enquirers were mostly met with an enigmatic wall of silence. On the whole this only went to enhance Kraftwerk's reputation as reticent and reclusive geniuses beavering away in the self-imposed exclusivity of their studio.

So, despite the overwhelmingly successful *Computer World* tour and a number 1 hit single in the UK, it was becoming evident that the public and critics alike would have little output from Kraftwerk themselves to compare against the new electronic music they had inspired. The three year gap between *Man Machine* and *Computer World* was now matched by an equally lengthy period of apparent inaction.

This silence was broken briefly in July 1983 when an EP called "Tour De France" was released, albeit in an unco-ordinated fashion. Limited copies of the 12" had been available for some time previously, but EMI had delayed its general release until there was more news of a forthcoming LP. In the end they decided to release the track anyway, on 7", 12" and cassette single formats. "Tour De France" directly reflected the interest that the group had developed in cycling, although opinions seem to vary as to exactly how this interest had come about. Schult maintains that following the physical effort of the *Computer World* tour, they had sat down and discussed the issue of exercise. Hütter and Schneider were impressed by Schult's apparent stamina and how he always seemed to be the one who would go to bed latest and get up the earliest. Schult says that he explained to them that he had taken up cycling and become a vegetarian and as a result Hütter and Schneider promptly did likewise.

Maxime Schmitt sees it a bit differently. He maintains that Hütter had always shown a keen interest in sport, going to football matches and even playing golf. At the time he was apparently on the look out for something that would give him more exercise. However, neither golf nor football really seemed to fit in with the Kraftwerk image. In the meantime Hütter took to jogging as a way of keeping fit. Schmitt remembers accompanying Hütter on his round of golf by cycling around the course on his bike. A few weeks later, Hütter rang Schmitt to inform him that he had taken up cycling.

Whatever the reason for adopting the bicycle, it wasn't long before the whole group were engrossed in it as an activity. Soon they started meeting at a cycle club in Düsseldorf and had nicknamed themselves "Radsportgruppe Schneider" ("The Schneider Cyclist Club"). It was evident that cycling was a good way of distancing themselves from the whole business of being in a group and the rather claustrophobic atmosphere of being in the studio all the time. Maxime Schmitt:

> "The bicycle was a perfect way of getting a lot of fresh air. Also we noticed that it was an anti-stress sport because it concentrated totally on the bicycle. When you ride a bicycle, you don't think about the new album, about how we are going to launch it. We realised that during three or four hours on the bicycle, we were discussing things like, "Oh, you have new brakes", "Oh, where did you get your handlebars", "Is the saddle well adjusted?", or "What about the pedals?", things that were only connected with cycling.
>
> On cycling trips, we would wear all the same clothes as the professional cyclists. When we met them on the road, they couldn't understand us. They would say, "It is my job, why are *you* doing it?" But to us, we had to respect this aesthetic."[1]

Having taken up cycling, inevitably the group looked for ways of conceptually justifying it as fitting in with their image. Just like the black stage gear, they would wear totally black cycling gear. On trips in the countryside, people were apt to comment on the rather intimidating sight of a large group of people, dressed all in black, cycling past them. Black clothes they felt reflected night, when most of their music was recorded, and also the colour of coffee, which the group drank in abundance when discussing their music. The bicycle was a form of transport that couldn't go backwards, so conceptually it seemed very apt for a group whose musical philosophy was the same. Lastly, in aesthetic terms there was the fascination of the comparison between the ever-turning wheels of their bicycles during the day, and non-stop revolving of the spools on their tape machines in the studio at night.

So, having immersed themselves in the technological imagery of the motor car, radioactivity and trains in the '70s, by the '80s Kraftwerk were reflecting the dawning of a new more environmentally aware age by adopting the bicycle. This meant that they had to engage in a certain amount of rethinking about their attitude toward technology. Ralf Hütter:

"After the modern world (trains, motorways, radio-activity, etc.) and the machines from *Computer World* we want to glorify the muscles of the human being, all this physical side. "Tour De France" announces a new time/era of Kraftwerk."[2]

Once they had got to grips with the bicycle as an integral part of the Kraftwerk ideology, it wasn't long before Hütter was waxing lyrical about the part it was now playing in their sound. Ralf Hütter:

"The bicycle is already a musical instrument on its own. The noise of the bicycle chain and pedal and gear mechanism, for example, the breathing of the cyclist, we have incorporated all this in the Kraftwerk sound, injecting the natural sounds into the computers in the studio. Kraftwerk has always been a populist group; on our last albums we have destructed the myth of the genius musician (like Mozart composing symphonies as a child) and we have shown people how anyone can play the Casio, how to make their own music themselves, alone. Now with the bicycle it is almost the same - cycling is the most popular sport, everybody can do it."[3]

Some might say that their interest in cycling reflected the kind of mid-life crisis that affects many men in their mid-30's who become rather obsessively health conscious. Certainly, Hütter's interest seemed to coincide with his decision to stop drinking alcohol and become a vegetarian. It would also be difficult to ignore the fact that their interest coincided with a period in the '80s which had seen a resurgence of interest in healthy attitudes toward living, especially in America. After all, even the rather frail looking Andy Warhol had taken to working out in the gym!

Of course, cycling was also indicative of another of the growing concerns of the '80s – that of the environment and energy conservation. By choosing to focus on the environmentally friendly bicycle, Kraftwerk were resorting to the ultimate in human driven technology. The bicycle still represents the most efficient and cost effective form of transport in that it is not reliant on any other power than that of human legs and arms.

As problems surrounding global pollution grew, it was inevitable that the long-term environmental concerns about the motor car were going to have to be tackled. On mainland Europe in particular, many people were beginning to view alternative modes of transport as a forward-looking answer to the problem rather than a retrogressive step. Cycling was no longer to be looked down upon as the cranky pursuit of a few hardy fanatics, but as a solution to the ever increasing problem of traffic congestion and pollution clogging up Europe's major cities. As such, Kraftwerk's involvement can once again be seen at best as prophetic, or at least reflective of changing attitudes.

For a while the group took to the sport as a unit, and during their first summer of cycling together they were often given to extolling the phrase, "Tous à vélo!" (Everyone on the bicycle!) However, after the initial bout of enthusiasm, it was Hütter who remained most interested. Cycling now formed a part of his daily routine that involved coffee, cycling for most of the day, going to the studio, then perhaps a disco at night.

Kraftwerk's sudden immersion in the down-to-earth topic of peddling must have seemed strange to those who might have fully expected the group to continue in the mould of the technologically obsessed *Computer World*. But in reality the development of the sports bicycle is as highly technically obsessed as that of computers and at the very top level uses computer-aided technology. The complexity of the modern bicycle, coupled with its potential as a transport solution, was the perfect step onwards from the car of "Autobahn" through the train of "Trans-Europe Express", and was not really as surprising a diversion for Kraftwerk to take.

In fact, the group were conscious of making some kind of environmental statement, without necessarily preaching or trying to put over some kind of "message". Emil Schult:

"Germany at that time was under very heavy industrial pressure. All the time the air seemed to be badly polluted, that's why I preferred to go to other countries for the winter. If you have the possibility of making music and being a prominent person, you also have to take on the responsibility to transmit the right message – unless you just want to do entertainment. But if you want to do something more lasting – we always thought our work was intellectually more fruitful than a lot of other music produced at the same time. It was a conscious decision to keep it on that level."[4]

True to their words, Hütter and Schneider as well as taking up cycling, also abandoned driving around in their petrol thirsty Mercedes in favour of smaller, more environmentally friendly Volkswagens. Maxime Schmitt:

"They all have small cars, as a point of respect to the environmental crisis. It's their socialist side. They used to have Volkswagen "Beetles" as cult items, and now they have returned to Volkswagen Golfs..."[5]

In any event, musically the sum total of the interest in cycling was represented on the "Tour De France" EP. Initially Hütter and Schmitt tried to persuade the group that they should do a whole LP based around cycling/sport. However, the rest of the group were not so convinced and the idea became focussed into a single track. The initial phrases for the lyrics had apparently been scribbled on a restaurant tablecloth. From there it grew into a song of which there has never been a definitive version. There are a number of different versions in existence, including two German mixes, a New York club mix (again with versions in French and German) and a remix in England, as well as an instrumental version called "2e Étape". The club mix accentuated the track's bicycle noises and breathy delivery. The group refrained from recording an English language version as some of the more evocative cycling vernacular couldn't be easily translated from the French. Phrases like "pédaler en grand braquet" sounded rather clumsy when approximated to the English equivalent of "to pedal in a high gear ratio".

Inevitably, with the title's French connections, it was this version that became most familiar, and is the one they still continue to play live. Also, it was the French text to the lyric that appeared on the back cover of the EP. To the uninitiated, Galibier and Tourmalet might have seemed like the names of cycling champions and not mountain passes in the Alps and the Pyrenees respectively – passes which Hütter himself had already ridden. The lyric ends with the last three lines; "le vélo vite réparé, le peloton est regroupé, camarades et amitié" (The bicycle quickly repaired, the peloton regroups, comrades and friendship).

In typical Kraftwerk fashion, a lot of time was spent on "Tour De France" meticulously recreating a bicycle ride from within the studio. They incorporated the sound of a bicycle wheel turning and a bicycle pump. Hütter even tried running up and down the studio stairs before doing his vocal, so as to give the breathless impression of someone actually cycling. The vocal was eventually recorded on the studio stairs so as to achieve the right echo. It is feasible that they were influenced by a record made in 1976 by the French avant-garde musician Jac Berrocal called "Rock 'n' Roll Station" which also used the sounds of the pedals, gear ratios and bicycle bells. Guest vocalist Vince Taylor even sings the line, "Jac's bicycle is music to my ears".

Initially, Schneider who was most responsible for the ambience of such pieces, was unhappy with the track. Not only was he concerned about the music, but also whether the highly popular Tour De France fitted in with the Kraftwerk concept. Being distanced from the actual composing he was often the first to suggest alterations. Bartos too had reservations about the mix. Hütter, being closest to the music was often the last to respond to criticism, but eventually agreed to go to New York to remix the track. It was typical of the sort of deliberations that the group went through in making sure that what they released was in the best possible form. Maxime Schmitt:

"They spent many evenings together discussing things. They would talk very seriously for maybe 5 or 6 hours. Ralf would be very concentrated, Florian would walk around like a lion in its cage. Sometimes it was very tense and strained. I know that all groups have these sorts of conversations, but they had the added dimension of defending the Kraftwerk concept."[6]

In a weird twist of fate, during the recording of "Tour De France", Hütter suffered a very serious cycling accident. This had been potentially life-threatening due to the head injuries he sustained. In fact, he spent two days in a coma. When he came round his first words apparently were, "Where is my bicycle?".

Although he made a complete recovery following the accident, there were indications that Hütter's interest in cycling had moved way beyond that of a hobby. Maxime Schmitt:

"Ralf had a tendency to go too far with the bicycle, both in terms of distance and in strength or endurance. Sometimes we were riding in the mountains for 200 kms, having done two or three passes in the Dolomites. I would stop but he would carry on doing one more pass and he wouldn't get back until well after sunset."[7]

As a result of Hütter's accident, "Tour De France" wasn't actually released until June 1983, reaching No 22 in the UK charts in the September of the same year. However, this success was not repeated in France, where the track was released too late to capitalise on that year's Tour De France race, selling only 7,500 copies. The cover of the EP was adapted from an old Czechoslovakian stamp from the thirties, and featured the four members of Kraftwerk cycling. Apparently there was much discussion about which order they should appear in their own four man peloton. In the end they are in the familiar stage placing of Ralf, Karl, Wolfgang, Florian.

The video that accompanied the track was based around old film footage from the Tour De France in the fifties. It features former race winners such as the Italian Fausto Coppi and the French cyclist Louison Bobet being applauded to victory by avid supporters. Early copies of the video also featured shots of the group themselves on their bicycles. Apparently, Wolfgang Flur who was least taken with the group's new adopted sport, participated under sufferance. As Karl Bartos remembers, "Wolfgang hated the cycling, he was forced to do it for the "Tour de France" video, he hated that."[8] Needless to say, both the cover and the video reflected the Kraftwerk trademark of harking back to a nostalgic futurism of a bygone era. Today, they still feature parts of the video live, but interestingly not those sections featuring the group themselves.

Following its release "Tour De France" was used on the soundtrack to the movie *Breakdance*, again showing their increasing influence on black American dance music. This influence was evident to Kraftwerk themselves who found that on subsequent visits to the States, they were increasingly being asked for autographs from black fans of the group. In terms of sales, following its exposure in the movie, a remixed version of "Tour De France" made the UK charts reaching No 24 in September 1984.

Far from the trauma of his accident deterring Hütter from his obsession, following his recovery he threw himself into the sport with renewed vigour. After a while, it was evident that the rest of the group couldn't quite sustain Hütter's level of interest. As a result he tended to team up with other members of his cycle club, retracing the routes of famous cycling races like the Paris-Roubaix with its infamous cobblestones. Typically, when talking about cycling he stresses that he does not view it as a purely recreational pursuit. He takes care to emphasize its functional aspect, denying that he goes on cycling holidays. Ralf Hütter:

"No, it's not for a holiday. It is the man machine. It's me, the man machine on the bicycle. In the same way the music: Kraftwerk - the man machine.

Holidays are an alienation, a consumption concept. To relax ourselves we ride the bicycle, it's enough. We are liberated from holidays."[9]

Schneider, who also likes to cycle albeit on a slightly less obsessive level, similarly praises its qualities:

"Sometimes I cycle alone, or with friends. It's very good to regenerate, it's also good training for remaining still on stage."[10]

Karl Bartos, who incidentally still goes running everyday, like Flur was evidently less taken with the role of cycling as part of the Kraftwerk lifestyle:

"At this time we were very much into this health attitude, biking and running. It was mostly Ralf and Florian in fact. Ralf got crazy about it, sometimes riding 200 kms a day. Once I tried to keep up with him and I got exhausted. Florian was more lazy, he liked a glass of beer from time to time."[11]

Hütter continues to be obsessed by the whole world of cycling and he once even made a return trip to Paris purely to buy a particular component for one of his bikes. When on tour, it is now common practice for him to be dropped off by the tour bus to cycle the last 100 kms into whatever town it is that they are playing (except in England where Hütter is wary of trying to adapt to cycling on the left). Also, during *The Mix* tour, Schneider had a small collapsible bicycle with him which he was seen riding around backstage between the soundcheck and the concert at some venues.

Hütter owns about ten different makes of bike, all of which are either black or chrome. He often follows races through the Dutch TV coverage that is received in Germany. In direct comparison to the mechanical answers he gives to questions about the group and their music, it is one of the few topics that he will get close to being animated about. Patrick Codenys of Front 242:

"I've never seen his (Ralf's) eyes shine so much as when he is talking about bicycles and cycling. For him, the bicycle has to be built like a computer, piece by piece, with spare parts; the frame, the brakes, the saddle etc. It really is a world unto itself, both mechanical and technical."[12]

Codenys' wife Catherine McGill shares Hutter's interest in cycling having worked in a cycle shop herself:

"I met Ralf Hütter at the famous Dorian Grey club in the basement of Frankfurt airport, where there are these Technoclub evenings every

Friday. We of course spoke about cycling, Ralf told me he had a Campagnolo, a very famous Italian make. He also told me that he liked to go cycling in the region where we live. (The area East of the French speaking part of Belgium). I've often noticed that many people interested in bicycles and cycling are also interested in other sorts of technical things, like photography, or in Ralf's case, music. In the cycling world, the technology changes very quickly, lighter and lighter wheels or saddles. In that respect it's very like electronic music with better and better drum machines."[13]

More recently, Hütter and his hi-tech bicycles were even featured in a French monthly cycling magazine, which described him as a German cycling fanatic who had an incredible state-of-the-art bicycle. Perhaps at Hütter's insistence, nowhere in the article did it mention that he was in fact a member of Kraftwerk.

What is clear is that in Hütter's eyes at least, cycling is still very much in keeping with the Kraftwerk concept. It forms the basis of a daily routine which revolves around a cyclicar and repetitive pattern of his obsessions – coffee, cycling, coffee, studio, coffee, disco.

BOINGS
and
BOOMS

THE SUMMER OF 1983 WAS THE SCHEDULED DATE FOR THE RELEASE OF an LP called *Technopop* which the group had been working on since *Computer World* in 1981. The LP's title had been taken from a description of the group's music by Paul Alessandrini. (The original title had actually been "Technicolor" but being a registered trademark they couldn't use it). *Technopop* had even got as far as being given a catalogue number by EMI. Similarly the artwork had been prepared, featuring bold red lettering on the front and four images of the group members taken from the video clip to "Trans-Europe Express" on the back. The inner sleeve's images were taken from a performance of "Pocket Calculator" that the group played in the early '80s on an Italian TV show called *Domenica In*.

The LP was subsequently postponed twice more and eventually erased from the record company's release schedule altogether. For a group who were never keen to explain what they did, no reason was given for these postponements or the cancellation of a UK tour which was planned to follow the LP's release. A track with the name "Technopop" did eventually surface three years later on the 1986 LP *Electric Cafe*. Whether this was essentially the same LP, or whether it was the single remaining track from a scrapped *Technopop* LP was officially never disclosed.

Unofficially, *Technopop*'s running order was to have consisted of "Technopop" (one long track that would have taken up one side), a rockier version of "Sex Object" which had apparently been composed at a London soundcheck, "The Telephone Call" and "Tour De France".

Inevitably, there were a number of speculations as to why *Technopop* was cancelled and its replacement *Electric Cafe* took so long to surface. Some sources correctly stated that Hütter's cycling accident had delayed its release, others suggested that the group had reached a conceptual watershed and they were quite simply unsure as to where to turn next to discover the most up-to-date sound.

Both explanations were at least partially correct. Hütter's accident had indeed been a setback for the group, but also they were probably finding it harder and harder to devise ways of keeping ahead of the competition. Understandably, with the mass availability of new recording technology they were getting nervy that they might be gazumped by someone discovering a new electronic sound.

Refusing to be drawn on any such speculation, they merely stated that they had been continuing to work and upgrade the Kling Klang studio with the latest equipment, some of which they were now importing from the States. In fact, it was following their visit to New York and its clubs, that caused them to cast a wary eye on the developments in the US dance music scene. A lot of black dance records were now encompassing sequenced drum and bass patterns which had a light and syncopated funkiness, and a subtlety that had previously only been achieved by Kraftwerk. In terms of competition this provided greater concern to them than the previous UK synthesizer boom. In particular, they were worried that the success of Michael Jackson's "Billy Jean" taken from his million-selling *Thriller* LP was making their *Technopop* LP sound dated.

Not wishing to aid the competition may have been one of the reasons why Kraftwerk continued to turn down the increasing number of offers that were now flooding in. People from all ends of the musical spectrum were clammering to have Kraftwerk contribute in some way to their records. One of these was apparently Michael Jackson himself, who joined the ranks of Bowie, Elton John and a host of others who had approached Kraftwerk to become involved in some form of collaboration. It seems that even Michael Jackson was unable to entice the group out of their shell. Karl Bartos:

"Michael Jackson came on the phone around 1985/6 during the *Electric Cafe* period. He wanted to have permission to use the original *Man*

Machine multi-track, it was either for him or for his sister's *Control* LP. Anyway, Ralf and Florian refused to collaborate with them. I think they missed the point really. They are really self-contained."[1]

In any event, despite being too "self-contained" to actually collaborate fully with the Jackson camp, Maxime Schmitt confirms that Michael Jackson was a big fan of the group, and that Hütter had met the superstar on a visit to New York. Maxime Schmitt:

"Ralf told me that he went to see him in New York, in a private building which he totally owns. And the thing that Ralf told me which is really extraordinary, is that Michael Jackson had clones in the building, he saw three or four guys, and each time he thought it was Michael Jackson, in fact they were fakes. These guys go out in cars, and nobody knows where the real one is. A very Kraftwerkian concept..."[2]

Of course, what was actually said between two of the most secretive people in the pop music world can only be a matter of conjecture, but Schmitt thinks that it ended with a loose agreement to swop musical pieces. (It is doubtful as to whether this swop actually occurred, neither parties name ever having featured on the other's work.) Incidentally, when carrying such tapes around for people to listen to, Hütter had taken to transporting them in a plastic supermarket bag rather than a suitcase, so as not to give anyone the impression that he was carrying anything important.

Anyway, it was evident that Hütter was extremely concerned when it came to keeping abreast of the competition, and Michael Jackson's music in particular. He was all too aware that dance music was adapting very quickly to new technology, and as Kraftwerk liked to be completely sure of what they did, they felt it was not a good time to release an LP.

It was through Kraftwerk's nerviness about keeping ahead of trends, that they were now in the habit of playing their new tracks to selected people, and in particular club DJs, to gauge their reactions. One was Karol Martin, a DJ at the Morocco Club in Cologne, who had assisted Kraftwerk on the *Computer World* LP. Another was a DJ in Bonn called Boris Venzen. It was from these DJs that Hütter garnered reactions to the *Technopop* LP. "Sex Object", for instance, was more of a pure synthesizer song with a quicker beat than the version that turned up on *Electric Cafe* having had violin sounds added to it.

What finally tipped the balance in favour of scrapping *Technopop*, was that it had been recorded on analog equipment. The emergence of digital recording meant that if they were to keep up with latest techniques, the group had to rethink their recording process and update their studio accordingly. In an attempt to put an ever more modern digital sheen on their music, Kraftwerk entered a new phase of apparent inactivity which far outstretched previous periods of silence. Between the years of 1970 and 1981 they had produced 9 LPs including the Organisation LP. With the exception of the solitary *Tour De France* EP, the rest of the eighties would only spawn one new LP, *Electric Cafe* which was finally released in November 1986.

Just prior to the LP, in September 1986 they released a single version of "Musique Non Stop" on 7" and 12" formats. Released in Germany, England and the USA, the single was not met with much enthusiasm. The B-Side of the 7" merely had an instrumental of the A-Side, whilst on the B-Side of the 12" was the 7" version. This in itself was, and still is, not an uncommon practice, but somehow people expected more from a group as unique as Kraftwerk. After such a long gap there was a general disappointment at the lack of extra material – or perhaps people were putting off passing judgement until the arrival of the LP.

It was clear that much of the time had been spent partially changing over to digital equipment, but also, having set themselves such a high standard on their previous two LPs, they seemed to have embarked on some sort of quest to find a new sound. Consistent with a group who were now aware that there were ever more imitators working in the same field, a lot of time (perhaps too much) was spent putting the finishing touches to *Electric Cafe*. Karl Bartos:

"We spent three months in New York for the mixing, but when it was finished nobody was really happy with it. So it was done again."[3]

One of the reasons why the group had struggled with this new LP, was that there was no conceptual umbrella that encompassed the new songs they were working on. The title eventually came from a number of sources – most notably an old Marlene Dietrich film called *Café*

Electrique. However, as long ago as 1976 they had had the idea of creating an album around the sounds of the café; the percolators, vacuum cleaners etc. They even went around various flea markets trying to find old vacuum cleaners and kitchen appliances that they could incorporate into the concept.

The group were also keen on the idea of creating something around the notion of cafés because they spent much of their time discussing their music and business affairs in the local coffee houses, which had almost become like second homes to them. They also toyed with the notion of the world as a global café, but avoided the temptation of becoming involved in the sort of "new age" concepts that were now being attached to a lot of synthesizer music. Having become much more dance-orientated, Hütter was keen to distance the group from the sort of soporific type of music that was broadly associated with the term "new age". Ralf Hütter:

> "I prefer the original music from the late sixties and early seventies. I find
> Tangerine Dream and Klaus Schulze more original, and I think new age
> music did not develop itself on this side. Now there is a lot of functional
> music, like in the shops, in the planes, today it has become a sort of
> valium."[4]

The problem they were having with the concept for *Electric Cafe* was that they had only fulfilled one side of their usual equation. Every one of their LPs since *Radio-Activity*, had utilised both nostalgic and futurist imagery. As yet, they had not come up with the modernist side to the LP's concept. This inspiration finally came rather loosely from a book that Schmitt had read about Stanley Kubrik, in which he described one of the sets for his film *2001* as a kind of space-age café where the Americans meet the Russians. In the end, only the title track really fitted in with this concept.

Likewise, if the cover was supposed to reflect some kind of café concept, it was certainly not evident. Maxime Schmitt:

> "There is a gap between the cover and the concept, it comes from a time
> when we were seeing each other a bit less, and there was some
> understanding lacking between us. By this time I was not with EMI

anymore, so I was not able to travel to see them as much as before, I was far less involved, it was developed more by the phone in the evening."[5]

Whilst on the cover of *Computer World* the group had appeared as pictures on a computer screen, on *Electric Cafe* the group's heads were in the form of computerised animation by the Institute Of Technology in New York. The faces of the four group members were reconstructed like the sort of architectural profiles that were now available to computer modellers. The cover of the LP was a still taken from a video featuring this technique, made by Rebecca Allen at the Institute to accompany "Musique Non-Stop". The inside sleeve showed a stage in the preparation of how the heads were transformed into computer graphics.

Like many of the projects surrounding the group, the video had taken a long time to prepare. It had actually started as far back as 1983, when the group first approached Rebecca Allen to make the video for a track which was then still entitled "Technopop". Allen had come to their attention as a video artist who had worked amongst others with David Byrne and Twyla Tharp on their *Catherine Wheel* project. Meetings in Paris and Düsseldorf followed during 1984. The Paris meeting was arranged around the group's usual schedule of dinner at *La Coupole* followed by going to Les Bains-Douches. Allen also remembers that Hütter was in Paris to attend a bicycle race that was in progress just outside the city.

After driving from Paris to Düsseldorf with the group listening to *Autobahn* in the car, Allen was privileged to work at Kling Klang, on the proviso that she brought no strangers to the studio. She remembers being shown much of Kraftwerk's archive material which included all the old artwork, as well as visiting clubs with the group nearly every night. She was also at the studio long enough to witness the composing of the track. This was a rather unusual way of working for a video maker, as most videos aren't started until the track is completed. Rebecca Allen:

"I wanted to work with them by modelling their faces. It was the logical next step after the robots and they liked this idea. It was a real collaboration, and I can say that the music influenced the image but that also the images influenced the music. Florian was saying that it was the first time they had worked with a woman and because of that they decided to use a woman's voice on the track. He said, "Since you are simulating our faces, we are going to simulate your voice", and they did that with the feminine voice which says "Musique Non-Stop". Also, they simulated other voices in French and Spanish."[6]

After agreeing the general outline of the video, Allen returned to New York to work on the computer graphics. To help her, the group had sent over the four heads to the dummies so she could accurately recreate their images on screen. The boxes were opened at customs, and Allen then had the rather bizarre job of explaining to the US customs officials as to what they were for.

The completely computer generated video was finished in October 1984, Allen having overcome the technically difficult task of making the faces come to life. Then came a frustrating gap before the video actually saw the light of day – two years to be precise. Such was the changing speed of computer techniques that she had to reserve a special programme at the Institute to store the graphics until Hütter and Schneider were eventually ready to go to New York to edit the final version. In any event, it turned out to be worth the wait, as the video is still featured during the group's live performances, as well as having being shown at various video exhibitions. Allen's images are preceded by a section which features the words, "Tschak", "Bumm", "Zoing", "Boing" and "Peng", all appearing in a cartoon fashion similar to the fight sequences in the Batman TV series.

Rebecca Allen is surprised that considering Kraftwerk's status, none of their videos have been made commercially available. In typical fashion, Hütter has in the past talked about the possibility of such a venture, even going as far as saying in 1983 that all the albums would be made available on video format. But like various other book, film and video projects that have at one time been mentioned, nothing has seen the light of day as yet. However, a short extract from Allen's video has been used on MTV to advertise MTV Classics.

From their pictures on the sleeve of *Electric Cafe*, Wolfgang Flur and Karl Bartos are still very much in evidence, but just what their contribution was, remains uncertain. On the least informative sleeve so far, no-one is credited with the songwriting, or any instrumentation in particular.

Similar to *Computer World*, there are a number of other people credited, including computer engineers and graphic technicians. The familiar names of Emil Schult, Matten and Wiechers, Marvin Katz and Maxime Schmitt again appear without a mention of any specific contribution.

It was clear that some of the music reflected their hesitancy over the LP's supposed concept. Some might argue that this was quite simply because they had run out of concepts. Alternatively, maybe this time they wanted to present an unencumbered and less cryptic album. Either way, *Electric Cafe* is essentially comprised of mostly dance-influenced pieces rather than "conceptual" songs. Possibly, the idea of a "concept album" was becoming less attractive as it was still connected with conventional notions of rock groups. Due to their huge influence on the dance scene they obviously felt they were more allied to the growing number of techno and electro music groups to whom the whole idea of a concept LP was faintly ridiculous.

So whilst *Computer World* was specifically conceptual to technology such as the pocket calculator, the opening track "Boing Boom Tschak" on *Electric Cafe* explored the periphery of the sound of technology – being a sort of verbal equivalent of the noise of a drum machine. This gives way to "Techno Pop" with its vocal describing "Industrial rhythms all around". The only tangible concept linking the tracks together is the theme of using the title of one track as a lyric in another. So whilst "Boing Boom Tschak" contains the line 'Technopop', "Technopop" contains the line 'Musique Non-stop' which in turn becomes the title of the third track. All three tracks are rhythmically linked together, being heavily based around a subtly changing danceable drum beat, which is treated with various sound distortions.

All this gives the first three tracks a cohesive feel of being one piece of music (as had been planned for the aborted *Technopop* LP). *Electric Cafe* was the first new Kraftwerk LP that people could buy on CD, although no concession was made to the extra space available on this format. *Electric Cafe* clocks in at a mere 35 minutes, short even by LP standards. In the face of modern technology, the group were continuing proof of the old adage "less is more".

Side two's opener (or track 4 on the CD) is titled "The Telephone Call" and in keeping with modern technology, it is clear from the sounds that this is a digital exchange. The woman's voice (that of Schneider's girlfriend Sandhya Whaley) at the beginning states that, "The number you have reached has been disconnected". The track is also unique in that Bartos was confident enough to persuade the rest of the group that he should sing the song. Karl Bartos:

> "I thought it would be good to have someone else singing for a change. It is still a typically Kraftwerk piece with its mixture of funky rhythm, musique concrete and pop music. So, we took the sound of the telephone bell and made music around it."[7]

The track essentially appears to be about a person not being able to get through on the telephone to someone they are close to. For a Kraftwerk song, this has the strangely human ring of a relationship about it, but the lyric only goes as far as mentioning affection and not love. However, is it singing affection for the pre-recorded woman's message that tells him that the number has been disconnected? This leaves one with the eery uncertainty of whether this is a song about someone merely ringing a recorded message for affection and company. The track's distinctive telephone noises came courtesy of British Telecom, France Telecom and the Deutsche Bundespost Telecom.

"Sex Object" has a definite orchestral feel to it with its electronically created string section. "I don't want to be your sex object" sings Hütter in an unemotional and almost nonchalant sounding vocal. The track also features some electronically recreated slap bass and guitar, and for the first time shows the group partially reverting back toward the sound of more conventional instruments.

The title track "Electric Cafe" returns to the stock-in-trade harmonised coda with its vocoded vocal and arpeggiated synthesizer lines. Although a Kraftwerk trademark, it has the feeling of retreading old ground, or at least a nod in the direction of their past depending on how you look at it. Also reminiscent of their earlier LPs is the fact that there are really only two songs on *Electric Cafe* – "The Telephone

Call" and "Sex Object". This not only preceded the trend that "house music" wasn't really about songs but constructing grooves over which there was a simple one or two line melody, but it also brought them full circle back to where they had started – building up atmospheric pieces of music rather than writing conventional songs.

Electric Cafe continued the group's fascination with using different languages. Apart from the very obvious robotic language of the first three tracks, French and Spanish phrases appear in various places possibly to give the album a kind of latin flavour. So whilst on the respective releases "The Telephone Call" and "Sex Object" have English and German versions, in Spain the LP was released with "Sex Object" sung in Spanish.

Although *Electric Cafe* has the same modern sheen as all their previous recordings, it reflected current trends by being littered with danceable beats. The attention to detail and the staggering diversity of boings, booms and tschaks in the construction of the rhythm track alone, made other people's use of mere drum machines sound sterile in comparison. Because of this, it is a different type of record to *Computer World* or *Man Machine*. The warmer classical type melodies having been replaced by a harder more metallic sound.

Nonetheless the LP received favourable reviews, and it was clear that Kraftwerk could still cut it even amongst all the younger competition. As writer and longtime fan of the group, Biba Kopf wrote in his review in the *NME*: "The economy of Kraftwerk's expression has become their signature. In a world given over to the illegible scrawls of B-Boy Braggards, their modest autograph is something to be cherished."[8]

However, other commentators were less kind and saw the group as having to finally accept that they had reached a watershed and that everyone else had at last caught up and overtaken them. What this really meant was that Kraftwerk had finally been brought, as one reviewer put it, "into a world that had largely embraced and vindicated their social and musical visions".[9]

Even if others had embraced the Kraftwerk vision, it was still unlikely whether anyone could ever recreate the depth and precision of their artistic endeavour. For 15 years they had been so far ahead of the race as to not perceivably be part of it. But it is a simple impossibility to remain one step ahead forever, and by the late '80s inevitably they were now just one amongst a whole myriad of groups that were producing danceable electronic music. Having said that, as Kopf suggests, Kraftwerk were quite simply better at it. So, now that samplers were becoming increasingly available, most musicians had the same access to technology as Kraftwerk did. But of course this did not necessarily mean they had the same talent of building up sounds or writing songs on the computer.

Probably due to the increased competition, *Electric Cafe* didn't fare quite as well in terms of sales, reaching a highest position of 58 in the UK charts and only managing No 156 in the US. In retrospect the relative failure of *Electric Cafe* may have been due to the fact that, after such a long gap, people were waiting for yet another definitive conceptual pop product like *Computer World*. By delivering an album based around tonal quality rather than melody, Kraftwerk had produced another wonderfully minimalistic statement, but one which wasn't so easy to view as particularly commercial.

The more cynical might also comment that this was synonymous with an album that reflected an increasing writer's block or lack of confidence gripping the group. This wasn't helped by the fact that all the press opportunities, including high rating TV shows, were turned down. To this date, seven years on, it stands as the latest totally new material that Kraftwerk have produced.

The advent of new technology now meant that musicians like Boris Blank of Yello could build up his own studio and easily reproduce the same sounds and noises as Kraftwerk. In a lot of respects Yello took over, by occupying the vacuum left after *Electric Cafe*. Yello produced clean, electronic, European pop often using spoken vocals in different languages. Their biggest hit "The Race" with its racing car noises swooping across the speakers is an obvious follow-on from "Autobahn". The fact that other groups like Yello and The Art Of Noise were now successfully combining similar elements to those of Kraftwerk, obviously provided their German mentors with a dilemma – one that they may have yet to fully answer or come to terms with.

By the late '80s, dance fever was beginning to captivate the British pop scene. Kraftwerk was now a name that literally dropped off everyone's lips from the techno and house scenes of Detroit and

Chicago to the Pet Shop Boys, Erasure, Depeche Mode and a host of others. Their enforced silence almost seemed to stand in resolute defiance, as if there were no need for them to comment on the whole scene that moved from "techno" through to "house" and "acid house".

However, it also provided the group with the problem of what to do next. Two successive singles, "The Telephone Call" and a re-released "Musique Non-stop" failed to chart in early 1987. The 12" "Telephone Call" featured remixes by François Kevorkian and Ron St. Germain in New York, with a bonus track called "Housephone". The remixes may well have been brought about because Hütter and Schneider considered Bartos' singing on the original version as too pop-orientated and unrepresentative of the voice of Kraftwerk.

All the vocals, whether natural, and vocoded or electronic were usually Hütter's, so during the recording of the original they had Bartos sing the tune over and over again in order to try and achieve the right voice quality. The remixes, however, were only successful in hip clubs like those in New York. "Housephone" featured a loop of the words "dial again, dial again, dial again..." over a frenetic rhythm, and was typical of the new house music where repeated or sampled little phrases would appear throughout a track.

Both "The Telephone Call" and "Musique Non-Stop" were accompanied by video clips. Whilst "Musique Non-Stop" utilised the graphics from the New York Institute, "The Telephone Call" saw a continuation of the now familiar trick of harking back to imagery of the twenties and thirties, in particular the German expressionism of Fritz Lang. Filmed in black and white, the clip features each member of the group one at a time. Dressed in black, they are seen holding a phone from the thirties in a black gloved hand, into which they are either talking or remaining silent. Not only remarkable as a rare piece of promotional footage, it may well be the last time the actual faces of the group will ever be seen in such a promotional context.

The video was made in Paris, in a short exhaustive period. Maxime Schmitt:

"When we did the clip of "Telephone Call", there were two nights of work, during the second night I think I slept two hours in the studio, and I think I awoke when it was 5 or 6 a.m., and Ralf was still in front of the editing screens reading a copy of the daily sporting paper *L'Equipe*."[10]

This was typical of Hütter's stamina during both his cycling marathons and studio sessions. However, such was his sporting enthusiasm that Hütter was beginning to experience similar ailments to those suffered by cycling champions, such as fluid on the knee, as well as pulled muscles which were giving him a lot of pain.

As a result, during the promotion of *Electric Cafe*, Hütter was at the centre of another health scare. He was in England to give a press conference for the LP, when he seemingly suffered similar effects to that of a heart attack. He spent a week in hospital, the eventual diagnosis being unknown but some suspect it might have been connected with the vast amounts of coffee that Hütter was known to consume.

Kraftwerk have always surrounded themselves with artists and intellectuals whose ideas and conversation they found stimulating. Now, they added a doctor and bone specialist to these ranks. Called Doctor Willi, he is an expert in sports medicines and goes cycling with the group. Unlike many musicians who draw their inspiration purely from within the music industry, Kraftwerk continued to look further afield. Florian Schneider:

"The essence of Kraftwerk is not so much the musicians. Rather our friends who are from other fields like doctors, computer technologists, psychologists, writers and painters. In fact, I would say we draw our inspiration from life, it might be from impressions of travelling, a TV programme, a book, anything that's interesting, or even an interviewer's questions."[11]

By the end of 1987, Kraftwerk had once again climbed back into the cocoon of the Kling Klang studio to recharge their batteries, showing no willingness to break away from their shy and publicity shunning exterior. Many of their contemporaries were now fully embracing the rock business with MTV, record company hype, corporate sponsorship and charity records. However, the idea that Kraftwerk might be associated with a commercial product or hype was totally incongruous with the group's ideology.

Paradoxically, Hütter and Schneider were now two of the few remaining musicians from the late '60s to have remained true to the ideal of adopting an alternative lifestyle. However, although they had succeeded in avoiding a conventional way of living, they were also becoming increasingly shaded from society, sheltered by the intensely secluded and private walls of the Kling Klang studio. It was soon evident that following *Electric Cafe* they were beginning to withdraw even further into their own shell.

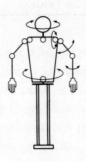

PAST
and
FUTURE

HAVING INSTALLED DIGITAL EQUIPMENT AT THEIR KLING KLANG studio, rather than recording a new LP, work started immediately on a project which would update their older material into a modern digital format. Perhaps as a reaction to the lukewarm response that had greeted *Electric Cafe*, Hütter and Schneider had taken the conscious decision not to write any new songs, but to prepare a kind of "best of" record.

As a result, the group dusted down their old analog tapes, and set to work sampling everything, including their voices, onto a synclavier. This proved to be an arduous task beset by technical difficulties. Eventually titled *The Mix*, the LP was to be 5 long years in the making. Karl Bartos:

> "It took a lot of time because the studio had to be rebuilt, the new synclavier came in, the 24 track tapes had all to be translated into digital. This was mainly done by our engineer Fritz Hilpert."[1]

Even with the extensive re-recording of their old material, the apparent lack of activity really did beg the question of what exactly did Kraftwerk do all day? For a group who in Hütter's words claimed to be workers and not musicians, no evidence of any new work was actually seeing the light of day. Hütter however was adamant that the group kept busy:

> "We work a lot. We all meet in the morning at the Kling Klang studio and we stay there throughout the day. We improvise and create new pieces. The very clean atmosphere of the city still stimulates us."[2]

However, during work on *The Mix*, it was clear that the increasingly slow progress was beginning to cause a rift in their ranks. The ambitions of Bartos and Flur were apparently at odds with the meticulous recording rate of founding members Hütter and Schneider. A lot of time was spent in the studio, but the Kraftwerk working schedule was perhaps not quite as rigorous as they maintained. Karl Bartos:

"We did go every day to the Kling Klang studio, that's true. On a normal day we would arrive between 5 and 8 in the evening, and we would have dinner and everyone would talk about what they had done during the day. Ralf always talked about how he rode 200 kms that day, and that would bore me to death. Hearing that for a number of years about these cycle rides. Yes, but most of the rest of the time we spent working, but sometimes we'd go to the movies, or go out for an ice cream.

But more than all this, I felt there was no force pushing us forward. There was no sense of urgency, all we did was enjoy ourselves. I was coming up to my forties and I didn't want to wait another five years to make a new record which would come out in 1995!

I felt as if I was in the middle of nowhere. Like with *Electric Cafe*, working 4 or 5 years to make 45 minutes of music - can you imagine that!? That's one of the main reasons I considered leaving, I thought with Kraftwerk it took too long to make a new album."[3]

Flur and Bartos were becoming frustrated that there seemed to be little possibility of any completely new Kraftwerk material on the horizon. Reportedly, Hütter and Schneider were in turn surprised by their impatience. Flur and Bartos were playing in Kraftwerk, what more did they want? The publicity shy founder members were at a loss to understand this frustration and were adamant that they were not going to change group tactics this late in the game.

In truth, Hütter and Schneider's stance may have been a wise and canny one as they were probably conscious of the fact that it was such reticence toward both new product and business opportunities that made the group so enigmatic and resilient in the face of changing trends. In simple terms it was preferable to produce one good album every five years, than churn out an average LP every year just for the sake of it. The group certainly were not going to fail due to over-exposure. Karl Bartos:

> "That's exactly the dramatic thing about Kraftwerk. All the opportunities were there and everything was turned down. I can remember saying to Ralf, "It's like I have this Jumbo jet in the garden, but it never takes off." So, I'd rather go and have a little Messerschmitt or a Stuka and do it myself. So, it's worthless if it's there and you never take it. All those people who wanted to work with us, and we never even did a soundtrack.
>
> We could have crossed over, become a big, big selling band. But there was never any management, not even on a small level, like two or three people. There was no telephone, no fax, nothing. And in this business if you need five years to put out a record then people forget about you. OK, it's nice to be honoured and to have a good reputation, and to be mentioned as an influence on all these other groups, but..."[4]

One of the reasons why there was such little product coming out was that there was no-one pushing Kraftwerk forward on a business level. Schult, who had been involved in some of the administration work, spent most of his time in the Bahamas, whilst Schmitt had left EMI and was therefore no longer as involved with the business affairs of the group.

This meant that all control and central decisions remained in the hands of Hütter and Schneider, who were notoriously difficult to contact or pin down. Most correspondence went through Marvin Katz, their lawyer in New York, but even then responses from the Kling Klang studio were few and far between. Hence some of the group's larger ambitions, like that of organising simultaneous gigs in different cities were probably technically possible, but physically difficult due to lack of willingness on Hütter and Schneider's part to let go of control. Emil Schult:

> "That concept could have been realised for a longer time if there had been the proper delegation. I think what was missing in Kraftwerk was the logistic organisation to do things like that. You have to trust a lot of people to organise these things, you have to listen to what they say, and not try to be the boss all the time. You have to consolidate, consult other people, and delegate specific work to specialists in order to make it work.

Otherwise, it's a bit like trying to make a film like *Terminator* all by yourself."[5]

A good example of the lack of organisation surrounding the group is the discrepencies regarding the availablity of Compact Discs. In general, some are available at mid-price, some at normal price, and others only as expensive imports, regardless of the obvious demand for their material. However, despite this apparent disinterest in maximising sales, their business acumen was sufficient for them to change record companies in the USA from Capitol to the West Coast based WEA.

As a result of the disagreements that were beginning to occur, Wolfgang Flur, after 16 years with Kraftwerk, was the first to leave. The last four years had been spent updating the old material which was mainly a technical exercise that required little direct input from him. Also, as there was no new material for him to play on, he had been spending increasingly long periods of time away from the studio. Therefore he clocked out of Kling Klang for the last time, even though according to Karl Bartos he was considered to be the heart-throb of the group, or as he puts it, "he was the cutist one, the girls loved him."[6]

In February 1990 the group played five selected low-key dates in Italy, with Flur replaced by their engineer Fritz Hilpert. The gigs were intended to be a trial run for a later tour, but it was obvious that the atmosphere was becoming strained. Schneider in particular was apparently increasingly uncomfortable with his role as stage performer. Maxime Schmitt:

> "The only time when they really have a professional life is when they are on the road, and they hate that. To put them on the road is an emotional drama for everyone, something terrible, especially for Florian who is usually impossible to find for a few days before a tour begins. Everyone has big depressive crises."[7]

In fact, Schneider's dislike of live work goes back a long way, as early as 1976 he was quoted as saying, "Sometimes I loathe all this on stage, it's so hard. There is too much noise, but it affects me in a sado-masochist fashion."[8]

With Flur already having departed, Karl Bartos, after much deliberation, took the decision to leave in August 1990 whilst *The Mix* project was coming to its conclusion. Obviously, the decision was not easy to make, but in the end the realisation that he had spent the last 10 years with only two LPs to show for it was just too much for him to bear, even if he was, in his own words, leaving "the best German group ever".[9]

Emil Schult's position as the hidden member of the band had also become increasingly fluid. His only contribution to the *Electric Cafe* album had been the layout, whilst most of his time since 1982 had been spent with his wife and two daughters at their home in the Bahamas whose former owners included Bob Marley and Grace Jones. He had become friendly with other Nassau residents Robert Palmer and Chris Blackwell, as well as former Talking Heads members Chris Frantz and Tina Weymouth.

He has continued to paint, and has recently moved back to Düsseldorf where in December 1992 he had an exhibition of his work shown at the Galerie Kontraste called *Colour Compositions and Underwater Motifs*. However, throughout the '80s he would still ring up the group and enquire if there was anything that he could do. Emil Schult:

"After 1982 I would come to Germany and work on ongoing projects or realise ideas, but they would never request me, so I presumed that was it. Then I heard in 1990 that they were going to bring out *The Mix* compilation, so I designed a cover for the album in Nassau which I thought was very good. It had features from all the old albums on it, but mixed together; the Trans-Europe Express going across, the bicycles and the Volkswagen. But Ralf and Florian didn't react to it, they didn't say come and see us, so I assumed that there was no interest.

Anyway, I wasn't sure about *The Mix*. Would Leonardo Da Vinci have taken the Mona Lisa back and paint her over? I guess not. "Autobahn" didn't need a remix by Kraftwerk."[10]

Never having officially been a member of the group, he hasn't so much left as stopped contributing. He describes the current situation as being one of, "They know my telephone number, and I know theirs."[11] In any event Schult continues to work with Wolfgang Flur on the interior design company they formed whilst waiting for something new to happen with Kraftwerk. Bartos meanwhile started his own project called Elektric Music and moved to a studio of the same name in Düsseldorf.

The new group was initially to be called "Das Klang Institut" (The Institute of Sound) but this was obviously dropped as being too similar to the name of the Kraftwerk studio, although Bartos still uses the nickname "The Institute" when talking about his new project. Elektric Music is in essence run by Karl Bartos and Lothar Manteuffel from the German group Rheingold, in collaboration with Wolfgang Flur and Emil Schult.

Initially, Bartos found that some of the doors that had been open to him as a member of Kraftwerk were now closed. Many of his contacts in the music business like François Kevorkian probably found it difficult to relate to him as a separate entity outside of Kraftwerk. But soon, his reputation as a musician in his own right meant that the telephone started ringing with people wanting production work done or wanting to collaborate with him. He has been invited over to New York to visit the Tommy Boy label, as well as being asked to talk about music production at the New York Music Seminar alongside such noted producers as Frankie Knuckles.

Elektric Music recently signed a recording deal with the German label SPV and have already worked on mixing the English techno group LFO and the US group Information Society. They were also the only non-British act to be asked to record a track for the *NME*'s 40th birthday album, where various groups covered former Number 1 singles. Elektric Music chose to cover The Equals hit from the '60s "Baby Come Back". (Incidentally, on the same compilation, Ride covered Kraftwerk's "The Model").

So far, Elektric Music have released one single called "Crosstalk" which features the same electronic voice that was characteristic in Kraftwerk. A situation they describe as, "When we left Kraftwerk, the DLS (Digital Lead Singer) was out of work. So we asked him to join the new Elektric Music. He is just another member of the group."[12]

It is clear that Bartos sees Elektric music as a continuation of some the ideas that Kraftwerk worked on, and in particular the idea of a universal language, describing it as "Elektric Esperanto". Karl Bartos:

> "By the end of the '80s Kraftwerk was a paralysed giant. The inner structure didn't allow any new ideas. Our music changed just by breaking through that isolation and moving to new things."[13]

However, Bartos has conflicting feelings towards his leaving:

> "I am very pleased that I had the chance to be in Kraftwerk for 15 years, it's a big honour for me. It would be a contradiction to be bitter and proud at the same time. I still admire Ralf and Florian."[14]

He also says that "Sometimes we meet by accident in the street because our new studio is not so far from Kling Klang, and Düsseldorf is not a big city."[15]

There has been a lot of speculation about the relationship between Hütter and Schneider and the other musicians within Kraftwerk over the years. What seems certain is that musicians from Michael Rother and Klaus Dinger in the early days, right through to present day collaborators, have all had to accept that the group image is more important than individual personalities. After many years of collaboration, even Flur and Bartos seemed at times to have been uncertain about their position within the group's ranks. They often outwardly appeared somewhat distant from the inner sanctum of Hütter and Schneider.

Such tight control can inevitably lead to accusations of a dictatorial approach. Many other musicians whose only real sin seems to have been a singularity of purpose have been likewise accused, from James Brown, Frank Zappa and Miles Davis through to the complaints of high-handedness often aimed against classical conductors. Clearly Hütter and Schneider are no less willing to let go of control of their product than anyone else. After all, Kraftwerk is very much their baby and it is only natural that they should feel protective toward it. Maxime Schmitt:

> "Of course, it was something which was very strong in Ralf, it's obvious, but without it the Kraftwerk concept wouldn't exist. When something is as sharp and extreme as Kraftwerk, as defended as Kraftwerk is, it is obvious that it passes beyond a certain stage, because it also becomes paranoia.

But not as people because they are healthy, they rarely drink, or smoke, they are not the kind of people that need pills to keep them going.

Both Ralf and Florian have fundamentally the same approach, to live for the music, they are Kraftwerk. They will stand up for this concept heart and soul."[16]

However, whatever form this protectiveness takes, as regards the input made by other collaborators in the past, Hütter recently commented:

"It's an open situation. Maybe I'd forget to mention someone and tomorrow I will realise that I forgot this person or that person. Everyone is important in a certain way, even if it is for small things, it is a continuity."[17]

Hütter and Schneider are always reluctant to talk about the past, whether it be people, concerts or their music. Some might argue that this reluctance somewhat obscures other people's importance in Kraftwerk's history in favour of the main creative force of the two original members. Hütter and Schneider provided the initial impetus and have always been the conceptual focus that people identify as Kraftwerk. They have always stressed that the group identity is far more important than the individuals concerned. Bearing this in mind, it is perhaps understandable that they are protective of the group image. Emil Schult:

"It doesn't matter, it's like a tree that's growing, and according to how it grows it will get to be the size it deserves. The real richness of success or recognition is personal; what I know, what I can do, where I can go. I have more friends in the music business now, like Wally Badarou, that's the richness for me, these are the good things."[18]

When *The Mix* LP was finally released in mid-1991 it received generally favourable reviews, peaking at No 15 in the UK charts, and was perceived as a successful project and a unique way of presenting a greatest hits package. However, from the choice of tracks it can not really be conceived as a greatest hits, as many of their best-known songs like "The Model" and "Showroom Dummies" are conspicuous by their absence. Most surprising is the omission of "Tour De France", which having been unavailable on any LP, would have been a natural choice for a 'best of' compilation. Apparently Hütter's response to Schmitt's surprise at its omission was, "Yes, it's like that, it may never be on an album."[19] Instead they took the decision to include some of their lesser known tracks like "Dentaku" and "Metal on Metal". Apparently, the choice was dictated by the likelihood of their upcoming tour, which nevertheless featured both "The Model" and "Tour De France" despite their non-appearance on the LP.

Nevertheless *The Mix* contains many of Kraftwerk's best known songs spanning a wide range of their career, from a re-worked and shortened "Autobahn" to a new version of "Music Non-Stop". Certainly, there were risks attached in re-recording a proportion of their most popular tracks, in that if they failed to add or improve on the originals they would have wasted five years. This was obviously something that had concerned Karl Bartos:

> "Normally, if you do a 'best of' record, you splice the old tapes together and you put it out and you sell millions of records. But if you do the same songs, and take out all the real things that make them strong in the first place, then bingo...."[20]

Maxime Schmitt, too, found that they were reluctant to do a traditional 'best of' record, "I really think it could have been something if it had featured the tracks as they were originally, just so that people instead of having all the records, would have a Kraftwerk digest."[21]

Hütter and Schneider themselves were wary enough of the enterprise to once again gauge opinions on the finished product from various sources. Prior to its release Hütter had separately invited his DJ friend Boris Venzen and Jens Lissat, a DJ at the Königsburg Club in Krefeld, to the Kling Klang studio to play them the demos. Hütter and Schneider were careful not to let anyone have an actual copy, but just to let them listen in the studio and give their impressions.

As a result of these consultations certain changes were made to various tracks, in particular the vocals to "Radioactivity" where the words were made clearer. The group were concerned not to repeat the ambiguity that had surrounded the original version. This time the lyric clearly states, "stop radioactivity", as well as listing nuclear disasters like Chernobyl, Harrisburg , Sellafield and Hiroshima.

In general, the reviews tended to fall on the side of Hütter and Schneider, and endorsed *The Mix* as being a good summary of the group's career to date. However, fans and critics were as split as those close to the group, as to whether it would have been better to have left the originals alone. Inevitably, some people were less impressed. Didier Lestrade:

"This album is a mistake. People were waiting for the ultimate frontier album, and with *The Mix* there is the feeling that there are thousands of sounds which remain unused. Kraftwerk should be astounding, which is not the case here. Also, they should have remade old pieces like "Ananas Symphonie"..."[22]

Indeed, on first listening, on some tracks nothing seems to have been radically altered and it might have been tempting to comment, "Why did they bother?", especially considering the length of time it took. However, many of the older pieces have been totally reconstructed with new beats and sounds that update them into the 1990s. "The Robots" for example, has a much more dance-orientated feel, not sounding out of place when played alongside the most up-to-date techno music of today. Repeated listening uncovers a subtlety and lightness of touch that makes the whole project bristle with newness.

Flur and Bartos' absence is reflected in the cover design which features the newly constructed robots, Hütter on the front cover, Schneider on the back. On the inside sleeve they were to be joined by two new robots of Karl Bartos and Fritz Hilpert. In the end, they used two different profiles of Hilpert's robot to maintain the illusion of a four piece group. Reflective of the technical exercise that *The Mix* represented most of the credits on the sleeve were attributed to hardware and software engineers.

The new robots were initially going to be dressed dummies like before, but instead they settled for stripped down minimalist versions that had finished heads and hands but bodies which revealed the working parts of the robot. These robots were now able to "dance" with their arms, but strangely for a group who relied so strongly on rhythm they had no moveable legs. They were unveiled, not as you might expect on MTV, but on the British TV science programme *Tomorrow's World*.

The continuing representation of the group as robots was also something that had become a bone of contention. Both Bartos and Schult were of the opinion that the idea was rather dated compared with the sort of robot technology that was now available in Japan. In their eyes, the robots had outlived their usefulness and it was time for a change. As Emil Schult puts it, "Do kids really want to see Ralf as a robot, or do they want to see the new ones like in *Terminator*?"[23]

Karl Bartos is equally critical of the decision to continue with the robots:

"In the beginning I kind of liked the robots, because it was new, it was a good idea. But if you do the same thing ten years later it is ridiculous."[24]

Hütter and Schneider, however still felt that the robots had an important role to play in the group's image. They were adamant that all publicity photos featured the robots, so much so that they even arranged for all their old photographs to be collected from the Electrola offices in Germany. They saw the new robots as an important evolutionary progression. Florian Schneider:

"We are very glad that we have robots that can now move during the concerts with real gestures.

The image of the robot is very important to us, it's very stimulating to people's imaginations. We always found that many people are robots without knowing it. The interpreters of classical music, Horowitz for example, they are like robots, making a reproduction of the music which is always the same. It's automatic, and they do it as if it were natural, which is not true. So, we have opened the curtains and said; "Look, everyone can be robotic, controlled." In Paris, the people go in the Metro, they move, they go to their offices, 8 a.m. in the morning – it's like remote control. It's strange...

In fact, we have exposed the mechanical and robotic attitude of our civilisation. It's a philosophical problem, but at the same time it's funny, full of humour. The robots may be an image, a projection, a reflection, a mirror of what happens – I think people understand that. You don't have to explain it, I think that the things speak for themselves. That's one reason why I don't like to explain so much what we do."[25]

As a reworking and re-defining of their career to date, all the tracks on *The Mix* were reassembled with the help of Fritz Hilpert, retaining the essence of the originals but embellishing them with modern drumbeats and sounds. Having essentially been re-recorded all the tracks have a homogenous feel, unlike traditional greatest hits packages which tend to reflect the growing sophistication of a group. Also, they are not merely remixes, as most groups would probably have done, hence the title isn't "The Remix", but the tracks have been digitally reconstructed using sampled elements of the originals. Ralf Hütter:

> "When most people do a remix that means they take the old tapes to an engineer who does something with them. For us it was not like that at all. At the Kling Klang studio, which is the machine that we play, the studio is our instrument, our musical work is called the mix. All our music is transformed in digital format, all the sounds are controlled by the computer, there are no tapes anymore, and so the mix is like a way of making music. So the mix itself is like playing live. In principle *The Mix* is a live album."[26]

Clearly one of the major achievements of *The Mix* project was that Hütter and Schneider could now dispense with the laborious use of tapes altogether. They now had the whole myriad of Kraftwerk sounds and melodies stored digitally on the computer for posterity, easily accessed for any purpose. Just like any successful company, or body of art, they were now beginning to look at their complete works as a possible inheritance. Ralf Hütter:

> "We have transferred to digital all our sounds, all our memory, all the old tapes which were demagnetizing, and we have changed all the original sounds into digital format in the memory of the computer. Now all the Kraftwerk encyclopaedia is at our disposal, a complete catalogue. And one day when we have stopped or died, maybe someone else will be able to continue with these ideas and sounds and make new compositions."[27]

It was now evident that there was an ulterior motive to the storing of their sounds beyond releasing *The Mix* LP. Ralf Hütter again:

"Kraftwerk is permanent. Durability is a central concept in art. Our sounds and programmes are immortal. Thanks to the computer someone else will be able to continue what we are doing..."[28]

Following the release of *The Mix*, the group repeated the *Computer World* exercise of taking the studio on tour, once again essentially stripping the studio of all the equipment and reassembling it on stage. The idea Hütter explained was to present something that was halfway between a movie and a discotheque, a modern piece of multi-media art. Although this left the Kling Klang studio with bare walls, it does also have a basement which is like a museum with all their old equipment and synthesizers in it, not to mention a considerable collection of the group's archive material. Florian Schneider:

"We use the cellar to keep the old instruments and machines that we don't use anymore. We never throw away the old things. It is very useful to recreate the old sounds, either from the tape, or from the old machines. Because it's different, we can't recreate them with the modern things, the sounds are specific, and for certain compositions we must have this specific sound from a certain time. It's also the age of an instrument that gives it a certain tone, a certain patina as in the old movies, it's impossible to get that with a new instrument, it's like old colours."[29]

The group are careful not discard anything involved with their past, and it is interesting how Schneider attributes certain sounds to certain machines in the same way as a classical musician would to old violins, for instance.

The 1991/92 tour was initially intended to be one of the most extensive they had undertaken, taking in Europe, America and Japan. However, the tour never went further afield than Europe, later legs being cancelled – or perhaps postponed. Incidentally, on the European tour, the Berlin concert was postponed when the group arrived to find that the newly opened venue in the East of the city was too dirty. The gig was eventually re-scheduled at a different venue.

For the dates they did play, they continued to include Fritz Hilpert who replaced Wolfgang Flur as the main drummer in the group. They also hired Portuguese musician Fernando Abrantes who bore more than a passing resemblance to Karl Bartos. Abrantes was replaced after the UK tour by another of their engineers Henning Schmitz. Possibly Abrantes was a little over exhuberant – by both dancing and smiling on stage he was not in keeping with Kraftwerk's more austere image. Officially, Hütter explained his departure by saying that it was too difficult to work with him as he lived in Portugal. However, they continued to use his newly made robot as they did not have time to replace it with one of Schmitz. It was apparently easier to swap group members mid-tour than it was robots!

In any event, the fact that Flur and Bartos were no longer present didn't seem to unnerve audiences too much. Most importantly, the distinctive profiles of Hütter and Schneider were still evident as was the classic Kraftwerk stage presentation of the four members arranged in a semi-circle. As there hadn't been any publicity photos of the group since *Man Machine*, audiences may not have been overly bothered about who was now in the group and who wasn't.

The group played mostly to 2,000–3,000 people per concert, proving that despite no new material, Kraftwerk had lost little of their popularity. However, some concerts in more remote areas were less well attended, and at some venues there were complaints that the music was not loud enough. As ever, what was played live and what was stored on computer disc was a mystery, although in interviews Hütter was now stressing the new-found flexibility within their set-up, allowing them to explore and improvise within the tunes. As Hütter put it, "It's a computer system, each of us have the contact (connection), and can play inside it. It's really the mix we can change."[30]

Florian Schneider:

"It depends on the song. Sometimes, everything is automatic, sometimes we react to it and change it. For example, in "Pocket Calculator" all is controlled by the small boxes. I think that we have created and developed this way of making music, and everyday we learn more and more – it's not finished yet. It's like a midi-DJ or a midi-mix. It's the computer playing with the software, reacting and creating...

For example, the words which are sung by the synthetic voices or by Ralf appear on the screens, on the videos. They are also initiated by a midi system, it's synchronised with the rhythms through the midi."[31]

Dan Lacksman formerly from the Belgian group Telex met up with Kraftwerk after their performance in Brussels where Hütter attempted to explain to him how the improvising opportunities within the new set up worked. Lacksman:

"Ralf told me a few things about the way they work on stage, and how they have the possibility to change some things live. Everything is based on pre-programmed sequences (probably groups of eight bars) and they have to decide just a fraction of a second before which to play. For example, they decide, "Now we play pattern number three", and they activate a specific control. Ralf told me that it is very hard on the nerves because they only have a few seconds to think of what is coming next."[32]

Patrick Codenys was also at the concert in Brussels and gives his opinion of their live performance:

"It was really interesting to watch them live. I was able to detect many things that were actually played live. On stage they are like laboratory chiefs who control everything. Obviously Ralf is doing a lot of things. I think he has a synclavier with all the sounds on it. Mostly I think he starts and stops the sounds rather than actually playing them, except at the end of the concert when they leave the stage one by one. I see Florian more as a good operator, but it would be impossible to imagine Kraftwerk without him."[33]

The 1991 concerts had many memorable highlights, always starting with "Numbers", "Computer World", "Home Computer" and "Computer Love." The rest of the set rarely changed its running order and featured other material from *The Mix* like "Autobahn", "Radio-Activity", "Trans-Europe Express – Abzug – Metal on Metal", with the addition of "Tour De France" and "The Model". In keeping with the age of "Autobahn", the car noise at the beginning of the track now falters, sounding like it is difficult to start.

The newly modified robots featured strongly at the end of the set. When the screens were raised to reveal the robots, they used the old theatrical trick of flashing white light to enhance their actions. The robots' movements were co-ordinated by Gunther Spachtholz, the tour manager, from a panel on the right hand side of the stage. Perhaps as a precursor to a day when the robots might tour by themselves, they were given their own segment in the show naturally enough during the song "The Robots". If a robot tour is a realistic ambition, Hütter and Schneider must have been heartened by the fact that they were received with rapturous applause.

Once again "Pocket Calculator" saw the band leaving the safety of their consoles to stand at the front of the stage, each member playing a small hand held device. To the delight of the audience they even offered these out for people to play. Schneider sometimes even mimicked rock and roll posturing by playing it behind his back. As one reviewer put it, "Believe me, if you can pose with a calculator, you can do anything."[34] During the finale of "Music Non-Stop" each group member leaves the stage one by one, exiting with a sort of improvisation reminiscent of a jazz group. Schneider is always the first to leave, for much of the concert having remained even stiller than his robot. As to what purpose the folder he always carries off with him is put, is a mystery. Finally, just before the curtains are drawn, Hütter starts off a final sequence and sometimes utters a few words like "Goodnight" or "Nous allons danser" ("We are going to dance"). The group having disappeared the music continues while the robot voice repeats the phrase, "Music Non-Stop".

The Mix tour, having never got past its European leg, finished in Budapest in November 1991. It certainly can't have been due to lack of interest from the public that the subsequent dates of the world tour were cancelled. More likely a contributing factor was Bartos' assertion that Schneider had become increasingly reluctant to tour. Or it may even have been due to the fact that some of the reviews of the concerts had been rather disparaging about the lack of any new material and had intimated that this was nothing more than the *Computer World* Tour continuing 10 years later.

In any event, it seems that some of the dates on the tour went more smoothly than others. This was confirmed by Bernard Gely from the French TV channel TF1, who had travelled to meet the group at a rather hastily arranged gig in Lyons, in preparation for a broadcast the following week. Gely arrived at the concert hall to be met by Schneider, who had travelled to Lyons via the night train from Düsseldorf to Paris, and then the TGV to Lyons. Schneider had chosen this rather complicated route so as to sample the delights of the new TGV which he was enthusiastic to experience. Schneider patiently and amiably helped Gely set up the robots for filming.

When Hütter arrived by the more conventional method of the tour bus, Gely remembers him entering clutching the suitcase with the discs containing all the music. Gely found Hütter nervy and agitated, and when it came to discussing filming the band on stage and the robots backstage, Hütter seemed to freeze and it became impossible to speak with him. Eventually Gely did manage to secretly film a short section of the concert, together with some backstage footage of the robots.

To coincide with the UK leg of *The Mix* tour, a single of "The Robots" was released, accompanied by a video which featured the robots from the tour including that of Abrantes. For the European dates "Radio-Activity" was released with remixes by William Orbit at his Guerilla Studio in London, and François Kevorkian in New York. The anonymity of the remixing process which can now be achieved by modem data transfer seems to appeal to them. Hütter describes his contact with François "le croissant" Kevorkian in New York:

> "We send discs, or through modem we transfer data, and he works, because we know each other very well, we exchange ideas, we didn't even go to New York. It's immaterial now..."[35]

However, not all the group's contacts are that impersonal. William Orbit describes a meeting that he had with Ralf Hütter over the re-mix of "Radio-Activity":

> "We met through EMI, their record company. They were looking for someone to make a mix for "Radio-Activity". So I went to a meeting around last summer (1991). Ralf Hütter was there, I was pretty excited because I've always been a big fan of Kraftwerk. He was very warm, his appearance was incredible because he was wearing shorts! He was very quiet, he didn't correspond at all to his image of a sort of wizard of the dance scene. We talked, I played him a few things I had done, and the

stuff he preferred were the things I did for Nitzer Ebb and The Shamen. He told me he wanted a "dangerous mix"..."[36]

After this meeting Orbit was sent a floppy disc and a two inch tape by Fritz Hilpert. Hütter, this time more soberly dressed in a suit, then visited him twice in the studio when he was working on the remix. Orbit:

"I was able to see that he is a total perfectionist, he has this purity, an obsessive attention to detail, I liked that a lot. And also the fact that he wanted to be present. Most people just order what they want and that's all. We did call Florian up in Düsseldorf a couple of times and we played him the remix.

I spoke briefly with Florian and we discussed something we have in common. Like me, he is very interested in phonetics, the sound of language. He has a device which fascinates me although I don't know much about it. It is a device which creates a voice, something much more intelligent than the vocoder. He can type something into the box and phrases come out. In fact I think all the voices from the last album come from that."[37]

With "Radio-Activity" having originally been a hit in France, the remixed track looked set to repeat its success even though their popularity had waned due to the relatively poor sales of *Electric Cafe*. EMI France tried to persuade the group to supply a video clip that could be used on TV. Kraftwerk as ever declined, showing no inclination to supply their record company with what they wanted. In the end EMI somewhat exasperatedly used the recent video for "The Robots" as a rather incongruous visual accompaniment to the track.

Despite their reticence to provide a video, they were still prepared to indulge in some promotional work by giving selected journalists an interview. During the Autumn of 1991, French journalist and friend of the group Jean-François Bizot, had the rare honour of visiting the Kling Klang studio which is apparently protected from mail and visitors by secret codes of entry.

Bizot was the only journalist to be afforded a studio interview, due mainly to his longstanding relationship with the group (Bizot had helped organise the German Festival in 1973, Kraftwerk's first concert abroad). The result of the visit was an article in *Actuel* magazine and also a 45 minute special broadcast on the trendy Paris-based Radio Nova. The broadcast was characterised by Kraftwerk recording a jingle for the radio station consisting of the robot voices singing, "Ra-di-o No-va, cent-un-cinq"... (105 being the FM frequency of the radio station).

This is an everyday promotional activity for most groups, but for Kraftwerk it was the first time they had ever agreed to such a ploy, having turned down numerous advertising and soundtrack invitations in the past. A more recent example of this was the opportunity to supply the signature tune and jingles for the brand new French-German TV channel *Arte* launched in 1992. As ever they declined, even though the high quality of this channel would have been in keeping with their own high standards.

Bizot went on to describe Hütter as "well preserved like a robot, with a nervous leg which springs up from his cyclists shorts, the hair style always perfect, hardly a wrinkle and the voice still soft."[38] He also described the Kling Klang studio where, "only the machines have changed. The micro-computers are piled up on the racks in the blue tinted neon lights. Their studio is a futuristic factory which is every sound maniac's dream."[39] Bizot then says that the group enter the studio like monks getting ready for electronic vespers. Working for so many years regularly from 5 pm to 1 am, Bizot asked how Hütter and Schneider can meet and work at the same place, facing each other for 20 years. "We have a buddhist technique to stay patient."[40] Hütter explained.

Buddhist technique or not, they have maintained a frighteningly consistent and disciplined approach, which seems to have varied little in the 20 years that the Kling Klang studio has existed. In 1991 when asked what their typical day consisted of, both Hütter and Schneider seperately provided uniquely consistent answers. Hütter:

> "I wake up in the morning, I brush my teeth (laughs), I go to the studio, I work, I go back home, I eat, I sleep."[41]

As if tuning into the same pre-programmed message, Schneider echoes the same sentiment:

"I wake up in the morning at about ten o'clock, sometimes earlier in the summer, sometimes later in the winter, then I brush my teeth (laughs). First I read the newspaper, I go to the coffee house for breakfast, I do the little daily things which people have to do."[42]

Both claim that their private lives are "nothing special". Which is either to state that they really *are* that boring to talk about, or more likely is a polite way of saying, "mind your own business". As Florian Schneider says, "I think we lead a life which is fairly normal. But then what is normal? That is a philosophical question..."[43]

Neither of them are married, Schneider states that he lives alone but confesses to having "a friend... but these things are private."[44] In reality, Schneider lives in an apartment close to the centre of Düsseldorf, appropriately enough in a building his father designed in the sixties. Reportedly, he and his girlfriend have recently had a baby daughter.

Of the two members of Kraftwerk he has the more visible sense of humour. Maxime Schmitt:

"Florian is someone who is very, very funny. However, he has a problem with communication. Sometimes when you talk to him, he goes red for no reason. He hates tours, he hates planes. He needs to have fun every minute. If he goes into a café, ten minutes later he leaves, he eats his chocolate, drinks his coffee, then its, "quick, we go elesewhere." The words that Florian says the most are, "what boredom". He works at the studio until 2 a.m. and suddenly he will stop and say, "Ahh, what boredom!" But the next day he always comes back.

He is also someone who is very contradictory. Sometimes he can get ultra-paranoic, if he sees photographers, he will be off like a shot and you will not see him again for two days. But on the other hand on the day of the concert at the Olympia, he will go and buy cakes in the next street, or he will mingle with the fans at the entrance. In the concert hall, people will be saying, "Where is Florian?" and he will be at the entrance, seeing how things are going, how large the audience is."[45]

The more solitary Hütter still lives in the family house which he shares with his sister and her family. However, when interviewed he states rather confusingly that he lives "alone with friends".[46] Hütter sometimes refers to as his part of the house as his "bunker", almost like an alternative studio. One room he has converted into a large open space where the floor is black and the walls and ceiling are mirrors. This was an idea of his that goes back to his college days, and is possibly an attempt to create his own "Hall of Mirrors". In this room there are also large TV screens which reflect off the walls. Apparently he has a telephone which doesn't ring but just lights up when people are trying to contact him. To Hütter the telephone is a dated form of communication. He has even stated that one of the reasons they have never collaborated with other people is that the studio has no phone. Ralf Hütter:

> "The telephone is an antiquity – you never know who is calling, there is no image, it is an outmoded product which constantly disrupts work."[47]

In another room, his eight or so bicycles are neatly lined up on a chromium plated metal rack. In the same room is a wardrobe which contains only black clothes, so he doesn't have to ask himself each morning, "How am I going to dress?" Most people's opinion seems to be that Hütter is a solitary person who has few close friends. Karl Bartos:

> "He is very intelligent, he is very aware of what he is doing. He said to me once, "I live my life like a railway, doing exactly the same thing everyday." It's very hard for him to have real friends. I think his only friend is Florian. He does go cycling with a couple of guys, they go for cycle rides for 8 or 10 hours at a time. He seems to need the mountains. He goes cycling there for three weeks at a time."[48]

Certainly, the general opinion of people who have met them, is that they keep their distance and that Hütter in particular is difficult to get to know. Patrick Codenys:

> "I first met Ralf around 1988/9. I had two conversations of about an hour with him. He is not talkative at all. We spoke very briefly about machines and instruments, then about towns, design, art, and inevitably cycling. But I can't pretend that I know him really. In fact, very few people really know him I think.
>
> Florian, I met recently when Kraftwerk played the Ancienne Belgique in Brussels, we spoke a bit. He is in a way more open than Ralf. In

Brussels after the concert he was asking, "where are the girls...?" but maybe he was a bit drunk."[49]

The distance that they keep between themselves and the public, means that they are mostly able to walk around unrecognised. As Schneider puts it, "In the town where we live everything is very anonymous, there is little media, it's very provincial, there are no radio stations, no TV stations, no record companies..."[50]

Hütter does sometimes get recognised on his regular visits to techno discos and sometimes he is asked for autographs. When asked if he is worried about appearing cold, aloof and calculating, Hütter replies that, "It is more maybe in the head of people. Maybe it is the prejudice of a period of rock – pseudo warm."[51]

Schneider feels that the whole image isn't without its funny side:

"Many people forget that there are little things which are human and funny. I find that the robots are funny – let's say between funny and... It's like horror movies, it can be funny and it can be horrific or magical, it depends on your point of view."[52]

Just as it seemed that Hütter and Schneider were ready to settle down into another elongated silence – an interesting twist in the Kraftwerk story took place. In June 1992 the group somewhat surprisingly agreed to play a concert protesting against the building of a second nuclear processing plant at the Sellafield site in Northern England. The concert at Manchester's G-Mex centre had been organised by U2, who topped a bill which also featured Public Enemy and BAD II. After a secret warm-up gig at Leicester Polytechnic, Kraftwerk opened the G-Mex show, starting so early that most of the audience and several reviewers missed most of their set which was a shortened version of their "Mix" tour and appropriately enough featured "Radio-Activity".

Commentators backstage described Hütter and Schneider as "tight lipped" about their involvement in the venture, and it was indeed most uncharacteristic of them to agree to do such an event. After all, it would have been natural enough for a group who had already turned down Michael Jackson and David Bowie, to do likewise to U2. The environmentally friendly Kraftwerk were presumably enticed by an event which addressed the global concerns of nuclear power. They may also have felt the urge to reverse the ambiguity that had surrounded the release of "Radio-Activity" some 16 years earlier. Whatever their reasons for deciding to participate, it was the first time that Kraftwerk had shared a stage with another group since 1973, and certainly the first time that they had involved themselves directly in support of an "issue".

Kraftwerk have also agreed to participate in a multi-media project that has been proposed for the city of Barcelona. Only in its planning stages this is envisaged to be a cultural garden located on a hill near the city which will be a kind of artistic, musical and video theme park. Other contributors to this project already include Brian Eno, Peter Gabriel, Laurie Anderson, Phillip Glass and David Van Tieghem.

For a group who have been so hugely influential, few artists over the years have been daring enough to do direct covers of their songs. Aside from the numerous samples from Kraftwerk's records, there have recently been a few notable exceptions. In the late '80s Siouxsie and the Banshees released an album of cover versions which featured a rather unsuccessful cover of "The Hall Of Mirrors". In 1991, American avant-garde guitarist Gary Lucas recorded a very curious cover version of "Autobahn" featuring guitar and sound effects which was released on a German Enemy label compilation called *Knitting Factory Tours Europe 1991*.

Finally, 1992 saw the release of a record called *Possessed* by violinist Alexander Balanescu and his string quartet. The LP features an unprecedented five Kraftwerk cover versions on it. "The Robots", "The Model", "Autobahn", "Computer Love" and "Pocket Calculator" having all been arranged as pieces for the string quartet. This not only further emphasized the classical nature of some of Kraftwerk's melodies, but also highlighted the subtlety of some of their arrangements.

So, classical musicians could now be added to a long list of people who are quoted as having been influenced by Kraftwerk. It is a list that has included musicians from almost every area of music; contemporary avant-garde musicians, industrial musicians, synthesizer groups, techno, house, acid house, electro and hip hop groups. Ralf Hütter:

"The mechanical universe of Kraftwerk has been cloned or copied in Detroit, Brussels, Milan, Manchester, and even psychedelicised by the delerium of house music. You can define it as you want; sci-fi music, techno-disco, cybernetic rock. But the term I prefer even so is robot pop. It fits in with our objective – which consists of working without a respite toward the construction of the perfect pop song for the tribes of the global village."[53]

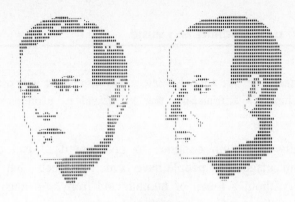

KLING
and
KLANG

FOR OVER 20 YEARS, KRAFTWERK'S DESTINY HAS ALWAYS RESTED IN the hands of Hütter and Schneider. Very little control has ever really been outside of these two core members. True there have been other musicians, engineers and artists involved, but it seems that within the Kraftwerk phenomenon, the central life-long friendship between Hütter and Schneider has, and always will be, the driving force of the group. Maxime Schmitt:

> "They are great companions, friends, mates. They never argue, never. I mean Florian will say, "Ralf is crazy", referring to the fact that Ralf rides the bicycle too much, or Ralf will say, "Florian is this". But both have fundamentally the same approach."[1]

They have often described their relationship as telepathic. Certainly, as with any two people that have worked together for such a length of time, an empathy or duality has grown between them. As Hütter somewhat humorously puts it, "Between us it's like the kling and the klang (corresponding to the ying and yang of Eastern philosophy). Schneider's friend Kuêlan agrees:

> "Yes, that's true. But sometimes Florian can be very ying and the day after very yang! He is laid-back, very feminine, very secret. I remember one day I asked him why they weren't releasing any records at present. He answered, "There is too much sound pollution."
>
> On the other hand, Ralf is very up-front. He is Leo. He has tremendous drive, very solar. They are very complimentary. Sometimes it is almost like there is a generation between them, Florian being the older and Ralf

the younger. They are not only friends, they also have a very professional relationship, it's a friendship that has found its expression through music."[2]

Outwardly they both continue to give the dead pan corporate answers and images that people have come to expect – but which in itself isn't without a touch of humour and irony. As musicians, or "workers" as they prefer to be called, they have reached the pinnacle of perfection, so it is only natural that they are reticent to give anything away. However, outside of the group persona they seem to have attained a kind of contentment that approaches aestheticism. Kuêlan:

"Both Florian and Ralf are exquisite, delightful, full of civility. They are almost models of the perfect citizens. They have a very refined European education. They are conscious of the past, the present, the future of Germany. They have a tremendously healthy way of life. They are practically vegetarian. They live in total asceticism and pay a lot of attention to detail. For instance, they even have their shoes made to measure. They are real gentlemen."[3]

Paul Alessandrini recounts one of his lasting impressions of the duo:

"I remember I had an appointment with Ralf and Florian at *La Coupole* restaurant. Our appointment was Sunday at noon, so it was early and the restaurant was empty. I still remember this image of them, sitting there all dressed in black, with their precise haircuts, their made-to-measure suits. It was like an expressionist picture, a very stylised one, the dummies could have been there and it would have been the same. I tell you, the girl I was with was frightened.

Also, they had become vegetarians since the last time I saw them, and they didn't eat the fish or meat which you would expect to eat in this sort of restaurant. They only ate vegetables like spinach. It was really a crazy picture – these two almost imaginary figures eating these natural foodstuffs!"[4]

Both socially and musically Kraftwerk's vision still remains unique. It is unlikely that anyone else could reproduce the oblique intensity and obsessive discipline that has enshrouded the group for over 20 years. To this day, Ralf and Florian still meet most days at the Kling Klang studio, their technological creation, their electronic garden, to cement and continue the Kraftwerk sound and vision. Even though some sources claim that Schneider is ready to call it a day (particularly when it comes to touring), in their own inimitable fashion they will probably continue to work at the perfection of their product for some time to come. As Hütter says when asked if they will split up, "we have tried, but it did not work. Our understanding is too stimulating. It is a necessary duality."[5]

As to what form, or when any new product will arrive, is kept under wraps like top secret company information. As ever, only the smallest clues are given as to what their future records might contain. Some sources state that they have been working on a "Mix 2", presumably incorporating the rather obvious omissions from *The Mix*. Hütter however has hinted that they may be once again working on new material by saying, "Europe can become a big multi-cultural society – that's what I would like to convey on our next record."[6]

Even in silence, Kraftwerk continue to entice and intrigue. In a media saturated world where we are bombarded with music, video and TV, there is almost something comforting about Kraftwerk's ultra-minimal approach. In any event, however long the next period of silence turns out to be, the music world would be foolish to turn its back on their laboratory in Düsseldorf.

There are very few groups or individuals whose contribution to modern music has been so groundbreaking, whose sound has been so unique to have started off a genre of their own. Many of these milestones are obvious – Elvis Presley, Chuck Berry, Phil Spector, The Beatles, Bob Dylan, Motown, Miles Davis, Jimi Hendrix, Bob Marley. To some, it might seem somewhat incongruous to place Kraftwerk's name alongside these luminaries, especially as they are the only name on the list not connected with an anglo/american pop culture. But for this reason alone they are remarkable. True, in terms of record sales, they may not have reached the same lofty heights, but in terms of influence they are equally important. It is simply impossible to ignore the fact that there are so many people in the music industry that fall in reverence at their very name.

For the last 20 odd years, the name Kraftwerk has been synonymous with an artistic ethic and lifestlye that oozes quality. Every record, career move, image change, has been so planned and executed with a precision that leaves many marvelling at the depth of their thinking – as if their whole career were the script to a conceptual movie. Some might say they were over-intellectual or cold in their calculation. But this is really just sour grapes. Who else but Kraftwerk could have produced the music that they do? Conceptually they have embraced every aspect of technology, both celebrating and warning about its use, producing a true "gesamtkunstwerk" or global art. They have investigated every conceivable notion of mechanical imagery, injecting a human and soulful side into their machines. They led the way in taking the synthesizer and drum machine to greater heights, producing some fine pop tunes along the way. The very word Kraftwerk now conjures up a whole myriad of intriguing and confusing images, an attractive and fascinating mythology which most importantly makes people stop and think.

To have achieved just one of these aims would be a considerable landmark. But to combine them all with a timeless, ageless grace that captivates people even when they produce no visible product, is awe inspiring. Quite simply, Kraftwerk have achieved *the* perfect marriage between man, machine and music.

AFTERWORD

We are in the year 2060. A few months ago Euro-Kling Klang, a town centre theme park, opened on the site of the old Kraftwerk studio in the centre of Düsseldorf. People come here from all over the world to dance, DJs come to mix tracks, deposit sounds and melodies in Euro-Kling Klang's massive sound banks which are operated and maintained by two permanently employed robots.

Euro-Kling Klang is probably the biggest disco in the world. In the main hall there is a dance area which is open 24 hours a day. Downstairs you can visit the Kraftwerk museum, drink coffee, and peruse everything related to the group's history. All their old instruments, robots and computers are still in working order, dusted and polished to a high state of cleanliness. The museum houses old video clips, even the orginal traffic cone that sat in their very first studio. Here too is Ralf Hütter's extraordinary collection of bicycles.

People can buy all nature of souvenirs, the most sought after is to have a personalized robot made of yourself which is then programmed to play your favourite selection of Kraftwerk tunes.

Finally, it is rumoured that this might be the final straw in the troubled career of EuroDisney which may have to shut due to the competition. Following the tremendous success of Euro-Kling Klang, plans are afoot for the building of a Paisleyland in Minneapolis and Madonnarama just outside New York.

Come to Euro-Kling Klang – for a sound experience.

SOURCES
and
QUOTES

GERMANY *and* IMPROVISATION
1. Ralf Hütter: Interview by Pascal Bussy, Lyons, November 5th, 1991.
2. Ralf Hütter: Interview by Pascal Bussy, Lyons, November 5th, 1991.
3. Ralf Hütter: Interview by Pascal Bussy, Lyons, November 5th, 1991.
4. Florian Schneider: Interview by Pascal Bussy, Lyons, November 5th, 1991.
5. Florian Schneider: Interview by Pascal Bussy, Lyons, November 5th, 1991.
6. Ralf Hütter: Interview by Pascal Bussy, Lyons, November 5th, 1991.
7. Ralf Hütter: Interview by Pascal Bussy, Lyons, November 5th, 1991.
8. Paul Alessandrini: Interview by Pascal Bussy, Paris, November 13th, 1992.
9. Ralf Hütter: Interview by Jean François Bizot *Actuel* Magazine/Radio Nova, November 1991.
10. Michael Karoli: Interview by Pascal Bussy, February 7th, 1992.
11. Irmin Schmidt: Interview by Pascal Bussy, April 13th, 1992.
12. Irmin Schmidt: Interview by Pascal Bussy, April 13th, 1992.
13. Florian Schneider: Interview by Pascal Bussy, Lyons, November 5th, 1991.
14. Ralf Hütter: Interview by Lester Bangs: *'Kraftwerkfeature'*, Creem (Sep 1975). Reproduced in *Psychotic Reactions & Carburettor Dung* (Minerva 1990).

SOUND *and* INDUSTRY
1. Ralf Hütter: Interview by Pascal Bussy, Neuilly, October 3rd, 1983. (Interview published in the Dutch monthly *Vinyl* in 1984).
2. Ralf Hütter: Unknown source.
3. Ralf Hütter: Interview by Lester Bangs: *'Kraftwerkfeature'*, Creem (Sep 1975). Reproduced in *Psychotic Reactions & Carburettor Dung* (Minerva 1990).
4. Conny Plank: quoted in *The Complete Synthesizer Handbook* by Michael Norman and Ben Dickey (Zomba Books 1984).
5. Conny Plank: quoted in *The Complete Synthesizer Handbook* by Michael Norman and Ben Dickey (Zomba Books 1984).
6. Ralf Hütter: Interview by Mike Beecher, *Electronics and Music Maker*, September 1981.
7. Ralf Hütter: Interview by Pascal Bussy, Lyons, November 5th, 1991.
8. Michael Rother: Interview by Pascal Bussy, November 9th, 1992.
9. Ralf Hütter: Interview by Mike Beecher, *Electronics and Music Maker*, September 1981.
10. Florian Schneider: Interview by Pascal Bussy, Lyons, November 5th, 1991.
11. Ralf Hütter: Interview by Pascal Bussy, Lyons, November 5th, 1991.
12. Jean-Pierre Lentin: *Actuel*, January 1973.

RALF *and* FLORIAN
1. Hervé Picart: *Best*, April 1973.
2. Hervé Picart: *Best*, April 1973.
3. Paul Alessandrini: Interview by Pascal Bussy, Paris, November 13th, 1992.
4. Florian Schneider: Interview by Paul Alessandrini, *Rock & Folk* Nov 1976.
5. Emil Schult: Interview by Pascal Bussy, Düsseldorf, June 6th, 1992.

AUTOMOBILES *and* MOTORWAYS
1. Lester Bangs: *'Kraftwerkfeature'*, Creem (Sep 1975). Reproduced in *Psychotic Reactions & Carburettor Dung* (Minerva 1990).

2. Florian Schneider: Interview by Pascal Bussy, Lyons, November 5th, 1991.
3. Emil Schult: Interview by Pascal Bussy, Düsseldorf, June 6th, 1992.
4. Ralf Hütter: Interview by Paul Alessandrini, *Rock & Folk* Nov 1976.
5. Karl Bartos: Interview by Pascal Bussy, Düsseldorf, June 5th & 6th, 1992.
6. Emil Schult: Interview by Pascal Bussy, Düsseldorf, June 6th, 1992.
7. Paul Alessandrini: Interview by Pascal Bussy, Paris, November 13th, 1992.
8. Ralf Hütter: Interview with Geoff Barton, *Sounds* November 1975
9. Ralf Hütter: Interview by Lester Bangs: *'Kraftwerkfeature'*, Creem (Sep 1975).
Reproduced in *Psychotic Reactions & Carburettor Dung* (Minerva 1990).
10. Florian Schneider: Interview by Pascal Bussy, Lyons, November 5th, 1991.
11. Patrick Codenys: Interview by Pascal Bussy, February 4th, 1992.
12. Florian Schneider: Interview by Pascal Bussy, Lyons, November 5th, 1991.
13. Karl Bartos: Interview by Pascal Bussy, Düsseldorf, June 5th & 6th, 1992.
14. Karl Bartos: Interview by Pascal Bussy, Düsseldorf, June 5th & 6th, 1992.
15. Ralf Hütter: Interview by Paul Alessandrini, *Rock & Folk* No 111, April 1976.
16. Todd Tolces: *Melody Maker*, May 1975.
17. Ralf Hütter: Interview by David Korn, *Keyboards* No 51, January 1992.
18. Ralf Hütter: Interview with Geoff Barton, *Sounds* November 1975
19. Karl Bartos: Interview by Pascal Bussy, Düsseldorf, June 5th & 6th, 1992.
20. Ralf Hütter: Interview by Lester Bangs: *'Kraftwerkfeature'*, Creem (Sep 1975).
Reproduced in *Psychotic Reactions & Carburettor Dung* (Minerva 1990).
21. Marc Zermati: Interview by Pascal Bussy, 14th May, 1992.
22. Florian Schneider: Interview by Pascal Bussy, Lyons, November 5th, 1991.

TRANSISTORS *and* URANIUM
1. Florian Schneider: Interview by Pascal Bussy, Lyons, November 5th, 1991.
2. Karl Bartos: Interview by Pascal Bussy, Düsseldorf, June 5th & 6th, 1992.
3. Ralf Hütter: Interview by Pascal Bussy, Neuilly, October 3rd, 1983. (Interview
published in the Dutch monthly *Vinyl* in 1984).
4. Emil Schult: Interview by Pascal Bussy, Düsseldorf, June 6th, 1992.
5. *The New Trouser Press Record Guide*. Ed. Ira Robbins (Scribners 1985).
6. Karl Bartos: Interview by Pascal Bussy, Düsseldorf, June 5th & 6th, 1992.
7. Karl Bartos: Interview by Pascal Bussy, Düsseldorf, June 5th & 6th, 1992.
8. Emil Schult: Interview by Pascal Bussy, Düsseldorf, June 6th, 1992.
9. Maxime Schmitt: Interview by Pascal Bussy, Paris, 20th August, 1992.
10. Maxime Schmitt: Interview by Pascal Bussy, Paris, 20th August, 1992.
11. Karl Bartos: Interview by Pascal Bussy, Düsseldorf, June 5th & 6th, 1992.

TRAINS *and* TRAVEL
1. Ralf Hütter: Interview by Paul Alessandrini, *Rock & Folk*, Nov 1976.
2. Maxime Schmitt: Interview by Pascal Bussy, Paris, 20th August, 1992.
3. Kuêlan: Interview by Pascal Bussy, May 14th and May 25th, 1992.
4. Maxime Schmitt: Interview by Pascal Bussy, Paris, 20th August, 1992.
5. Paul Alessandrini: Interview by Pascal Bussy, Paris, November 13th, 1992.
6. Ralf Hütter: Interview by Sylvain Gire, Paris, November 1991, broadcast on *France Culture* in "Coda" (Jan 28th - Feb 1st, 1992).
7. Maxime Schmitt: Interview by Pascal Bussy, Paris, 20th August, 1992.
8. Ralf Hütter: Interview by Sylvain Gire, Paris, November 1991, broadcast on *France Culture* in "Coda" (Jan 28th - Feb 1st, 1992).
9. Karl Bartos: Interview by Pascal Bussy, March 25th, 1992.
10. Karl Bartos: Interview by Pascal Bussy, Düsseldorf, June 5th & 6th, 1992.
11. Maxime Schmitt: Interview by Pascal Bussy, Paris, 20th August, 1992.
12. Richard H. Kirk: From *Cabaret Voltaire - The Art Of The Sixth Sense* by Mick Fish & Dave Hallbery (SAF second edition 1988).

MAN *and* MACHINE
1. Karl Bartos: Interview by Pascal Bussy, Düsseldorf, June 5th & 6th, 1992.
2. Ralf Hütter: Interview with Geoff Barton, *Sounds*, November 1975.
3. Ralf Hütter: Interview by Sylvain Gire, Paris, November 1991, broadcast on *France Culture* in "Coda" (Jan 28th - Feb 1st, 1992).
4. Karl Bartos: Interview by Pascal Bussy, Düsseldorf, June 5th & 6th, 1992.
5. Emil Schult: Interview by Pascal Bussy, Düsseldorf, June 6th, 1992.
6. Maxime Schmitt: Interview by Pascal Bussy, Paris, 20th August, 1992.
7. Maxime Schmitt: Interview by Pascal Bussy, Paris, 20th August, 1992.
8. Emil Schult: Interview by Pascal Bussy, Düsseldorf, June 6th, 1992.
9. Ralf Hütter: Interview by Sylvain Gire, Paris, November 1991, broadcast on *France Culture* in "Coda" (Jan 28th - Feb 1st, 1992).
10. Emil Schult: Interview by Pascal Bussy, Düsseldorf, June 6th, 1992.
11. Maxime Schmitt: Interview by Pascal Bussy, Paris, 20th August, 1992.
12. Maxime Schmitt: Interview by Pascal Bussy, Paris, 20th August, 1992.
13. Karl Bartos: Interview by Pascal Bussy, Düsseldorf, June 5th & 6th, 1992.
14. Bono: *NME*, 4th April, 1992.
15. Ralf Hütter: Interview by Sylvain Gire, Paris, November 1991, broadcast on *France Culture* in "Coda" (Jan 28th - Feb 1st, 1992).
16. Maxime Schmitt: Interview by Pascal Bussy, Paris, 20th August, 1992.
17. Karl Bartos: Interview by Pascal Bussy, Düsseldorf, June 5th & 6th, 1992.
18. Maxime Schmitt: Interview by Pascal Bussy, Paris, 20th August, 1992.
19. Karl Bartos: Interview by Pascal Bussy, Düsseldorf, June 5th & 6th, 1992.

CALCULATORS *and* DISCOS
1. Ralf Hütter: Interview by Jean François Bizot, *Actuel* Magazine/Radio Nova, November 1991.
2. EMI press release for *Computer World*.
3. Ralf Hütter: Unknown source.
4. Ralf Hütter: Interview by Mike Beecher in *Electronics and Music Maker*, September 1981.
5. Ralf Hütter: Interview by Steve Taylor, *The Face*, March 1982.
6. Ralf Hütter: Interview by Pascal Bussy, Neuilly, October 3rd, 1983. (Interview published in the Dutch monthly *Vinyl* in 1984).
7. Maxime Schmitt: Interview by Pascal Bussy, Paris, 20th August, 1992.
8. Ralf Hütter: Interview by Neil Rowland, *Melody Maker*, July 1981.
9. Maxime Schmitt: Interview by Pascal Bussy, Paris, 20th August, 1992.
10. Karl Bartos: Interview by Pascal Bussy, Düsseldorf, June 5th & 6th, 1992.
11. Karl Bartos: Interview by Pascal Bussy, March 25th, 1992.
12. Ralf Hütter: Interview by Pascal Bussy, October 3rd, 1983. (Interview published in the Dutch monthly *Vinyl* in 1984).
13. Ralf Hütter: Interview by Mike Beecher in *Electronics and Music Maker*, September 1981.
14. Ralf Hütter: Interview by Sylvain Gire, Paris, November 1991, broadcast on *France Culture* (Jan 28th - Feb 1st, 1992).
15. Emil Schult: Interview by Pascal Bussy, Düsseldorf, June 6th, 1992.
16. Martin Fraudreau: Interview by Pascal Bussy, Paris, 1992.
17. Patrick Zerbib: *Actuel*, March, 1980.
18. Ralf Hütter: Interview by Mike Beecher in *Electronics and Music Maker* (September 1981).
19. Arthur Baker: Interview by Olivier Cachin, *Rock 'n' Folk*.
20. Karl Bartos: Interview by Pascal Bussy, Düsseldorf, June 5th & 6th, 1992.
21. Boris Venzen: Interview by Pascal Bussy, May, 1992.
22. Karl Bartos: Interview by Pascal Bussy, Düsseldorf, June 5th & 6th, 1992.

23. Maxime Schmitt: Interview by Pascal Bussy, Paris, 20th August, 1992.
24. Ralf Hütter: Interview by Pascal Bussy, Lyons, November 5th, 1991.
25. Maxime Schmitt: Interview by Pascal Bussy, Paris, 20th August, 1992.
26. Patrick Codenys: Interview by Pascal Bussy, February 4th, 1992.

RHYTHMS *and* CYCLES
1. Maxime Schmitt: Interview by Pascal Bussy, Paris, 20th August, 1992.
2. Ralf Hütter: Interview by Pascal Bussy, Neuilly, October 3rd, 1983. (Interview published in the Dutch monthly *Vinyl* in 1984).
3. Ralf Hütter: Interview by Pascal Bussy, Lyons, November 5th, 1991.
4. Emil Schult: Interview by Pascal Bussy, Düsseldorf, June 6th, 1992.
5. Maxime Schmitt: Interview by Pascal Bussy, Paris, 20th August, 1992.
6. Maxime Schmitt: Interview by Pascal Bussy, Paris, 20th August, 1992.
7. Maxime Schmitt: Interview by Pascal Bussy, Paris, 20th August, 1992.
8. Karl Bartos: Interview by Pascal Bussy, Düsseldorf, June 5th & 6th, 1992.
9. Ralf Hütter: Interview by Pascal Bussy, Lyons, November 5th, 1991.
10. Florian Schneider: Interview by Pascal Bussy, Lyons, November 5th, 1991.
11. Karl Bartos: Interview by Pascal Bussy, Düsseldorf, June 5th & 6th, 1992.
12. Patrick Codenys: Interview by Pascal Bussy, February 4th, 1992.
13. Catherine McGill: Interview by Pascal Bussy, February 6th, 1992.

BOINGS *and* BOOMS
1. Karl Bartos: Interview by Pascal Bussy, Düsseldorf, June 5th & 6th, 1992.
2. Maxime Schmitt: Interview by Pascal Bussy, Paris, 20th August, 1992.
3. Karl Bartos: Interview by Pascal Bussy, Düsseldorf, June 5th & 6th, 1992.
4. Ralf Hütter: Interview by Jean François Bizot, *Actuel* Magazine/Radio Nova, November 1991.
5. Maxime Schmitt: Interview by Pascal Bussy, Paris, 20th August, 1992.
6. Rebecca Allen: Interview by Pascal Bussy, January 4th, 1993.
7. Karl Bartos: Interview by Pascal Bussy, Düsseldorf, June 5th & 6th, 1992.
8. Biba Kopf: *NME*, 8th Nov, 1986.
9. *The New Trouser Press Record Guide*. Ed. Ira Robbins (Scribners 1985).
10. Maxime Schmitt: Interview by Pascal Bussy, Paris, 20th August, 1992.
11. Florian Schneider: Interview by Pascal Bussy, Lyons, November 5th, 1991.

PAST *and* FUTURE
1. Karl Bartos: Interview by Pascal Bussy, March 25th, 1992.
2. Ralf Hütter: Interview by Pascal Bussy, Neuilly, October 3rd, 1983. (Interview published in the Dutch monthly *Vinyl* in 1984).
3. Karl Bartos: Interview by Pascal Bussy, Düsseldorf, June 5th & 6th, 1992.
4. Karl Bartos: Interview by Pascal Bussy, Düsseldorf, June 5th & 6th, 1992.
5. Emil Schult: Interview by Pascal Bussy, Düsseldorf, June 6th, 1992.
6. Karl Bartos: Interview by Pascal Bussy, Düsseldorf, June 5th & 6th, 1992.
7. Maxime Schmitt: Interview by Pascal Bussy, Paris, 20th August, 1992.
8 Florian Schneider: Interview by Paul Alessandrini, *Rock & Folk*, Nov 1976.
9 Karl Bartos: Interview by Pascal Bussy, Düsseldorf, June 5th & 6th, 1992.
10. Emil Schult: Interview by Pascal Bussy, Düsseldorf, June 6th, 1992.
11. Emil Schult: Interview by Pascal Bussy, Düsseldorf, June 6th, 1992.
12. Karl Bartos: Promotional interview by Stefan Ingmann, January 1993.
13. Karl Bartos: Promotional interview by Stefan Ingmann, January 1993.
14. Karl Bartos: Interview by Pascal Bussy, Düsseldorf, June 5th & 6th, 1992.
15. Karl Bartos: Interview by Pascal Bussy, Düsseldorf, June 5th & 6th, 1992.
16. Maxime Schmitt: Interview by Pascal Bussy, Paris, 20th August, 1992.
17. Ralf Hütter: Interview by Pascal Bussy, Lyons, November 5th, 1991.

18. Emil Schult: Interview by Pascal Bussy, Düsseldorf, June 6th, 1992.
19. Maxime Schmitt: Interview by Pascal Bussy, Paris, 20th August, 1992.
20. Karl Bartos: Interview by Pascal Bussy, Düsseldorf, June 5th & 6th, 1992.
21. Maxime Schmitt: Interview by Pascal Bussy, Paris, 20th August, 1992.
22. Didier Lestrade: Interview by Pascal Bussy, 20th March, 1992.
23. Emil Schult: Interview by Pascal Bussy, Düsseldorf, June 6th, 1992.
24. Karl Bartos: Interview by Pascal Bussy, Düsseldorf, June 5th & 6th, 1992.
25. Florian Schneider: Interview by Pascal Bussy, Lyons, November 5th, 1991.
26. Ralf Hütter: Interview by Pascal Bussy, Lyons, November 5th, 1991.
27. Ralf Hütter: Interview by Sylvain Gire, Paris, November 1991, broadcast on *France Culture* in "Coda" (Jan 28th - Feb 1st, 1992).
28. Ralf Hütter: Interview by David Korn, *Keyboards* No 51, January 1992.
29. Florian Schneider: Interview by Pascal Bussy, Lyons, November 5th, 1991.
30. Ralf Hütter: Interview by Pascal Bussy, Lyons, November 5th, 1991.
31. Florian Schneider: Interview by Pascal Bussy, Lyons, November 5th, 1991.
32. Dan Lacksman: Interview by Pascal Bussy, May 15th, 1992.
33. Patrick Codenys: Interview by Pascal Bussy, February 4th, 1992.
34. David Quantick: *NME* 3rd August, 1991.
35. Ralf Hütter: Interview by Pascal Bussy, Lyons, November 5th, 1991.
36. William Orbit: Interview by Pascal Bussy, March 25th, 1992.
37. William Orbit: Interview by Pascal Bussy, March 25th, 1992.
38. Jean François Bizot, *Actuel* Magazine/Radio Nova, November 1991.
39. Jean François Bizot, *Actuel* Magazine/Radio Nova, November 1991.
40. Ralf Hütter: Interview by Jean François Bizot, *Actuel* Magazine/Radio Nova, November 1991.
41. Ralf Hütter: Interview by Pascal Bussy, Lyons, November 5th, 1991.
42. Florian Schneider: Interview by Pascal Bussy, Lyons, November 5th, 1991.
43. Florian Schneider: Interview by Pascal Bussy, Lyons, November 5th, 1991.
44. Florian Schneider: Interview by Pascal Bussy, Lyons, November 5th, 1991.
45. Maxime Schmitt: Interview by Pascal Bussy, Paris, 20th August, 1992.
46. Ralf Hütter: Interview by Pascal Bussy, Lyons, November 5th, 1991.
47. Ralf Hütter: Interview by Didier Lestrade, *Libération*, Nov 12th, 1991.
48. Karl Bartos: Interview by Pascal Bussy, Düsseldorf, June 5th & 6th, 1992.
49. Patrick Codenys: Interview by Pascal Bussy, February 4th, 1992.
50. Florian Schneider: Interview by Pascal Bussy, Lyons, November 5th, 1991.
51. Ralf Hütter: Interview by Pascal Bussy, Lyons, November 5th, 1991.
52. Florian Schneider: Interview by Pascal Bussy, Lyons, November 5th, 1991.
53. Ralf Hütter: Interview by Andrea Petrini, *Lyon Libération*, November 5th, 1991.

KLING *and* KLANG
1. Maxime Schmitt: Interview by Pascal Bussy, Paris, 20th August, 1992.
2. Kuêlan: Interview by Pascal Bussy, May 14th and May 25th, 1992.
3. Kuêlan: Interview by Pascal Bussy, May 14th and May 25th, 1992.
4. Paul Alessandrini: Interview by Pascal Bussy, Paris, November 13th, 1992.
5. Ralf Hütter: Interview with Paul Alessandrini, *Rock & Folk*, November 1976.
6. Ralf Hütter: Interview by Jean François Bizot, *Actuel* Magazine/Radio Nova, November 1991.

DISCOGRAPHY

The following discography includes a list of the original LP releases, and the equivalent relevant UK releases as well as notable foreign releases.
For the singles we have listed the German and UK releases as well as notable foreign releases. Many of the singles have been released in different countries and in different formats/versions/edit/re-mixes in promotional form or white label DJ format and are too numerous to mention. There are also a considerable amount of bootleg LPs/CDs available which we have chosen not to endorse by including them in this listing.
In compiling this listing, we are greatly indebted to discography listings in *Record Collector* and *Cyber Noise* magazines. We are especially indebted to Ian Calder for supplying us with his exhaustive list of releases.

LPs

ORGANISATION – TONE FLOAT (RCA SF8111) (UK release)
Side One: Tone Float
Side Two: Milk Rock, Silver Forest, Rhythm Salad, Noitasinagro

KRAFTWERK 1 (Philips 6305 058)
Side One: Ruckzuck, Stratovarius
Side Two: Megaherz, Vom Himmel Hoch
Reissued in 1975 in single sleeve (Philips 6305 058)

KRAFTWERK 2 (Philips 6305 117)
Side One: Klingklang, Atem
Side Two: Strom, Spule 4, Wellenlänge, Harmonika
Reissued in 1975 in a single sleeve (Philips 6305 117)

RALF UND FLORIAN (Ralf and Florian) (Philips 6305 197 D)
Side One: Elektrisches Roulette, Tongebirge, Kristallo, Heimatklänge
Side Two: Tanzmusik, Ananas Symphonie
Initial copies contained free comic
Released in a different sleeve the UK (Vertigo 6360 616)
Released in the U.S. (Vertigo VEL 2006)

AUTOBAHN (Philips 6305 231)
Side One: Autobahn
Side Two: Kometenmelodie 1, Kometenmelodie 2, Mitternacht, Morgenspaziergang
Released in the UK (Vertigo 6360 620)
Reissued in Germany in 1985 (EMI 2400 701)
Reissued in UK 1985 CD/LP/MC (EMI Auto 1)
Current European CD (EMI CDP 7 461532)

RADIO-AKTIVITÄT (Radioactivity)(Kling Klang 06482 087)
Side One: Geigerzähler (Geiger Counter), Radioaktvität (Radioctivity), Radioland, Ätherwellen (Airwaves), Sendepause (Intermission), Nachrichten (News).
Side Two: Die Stimme Der Energie (The Voice of Energy), Antenne (Antenna), Radio Sterne (Radio Stars), Uran (Uranium), Transistor, Ohm Sweet Ohm.
Early copies contained free stickers
Released in the UK as Radioactivity (Capitol EST 11457)
Re-issued in 1982 in the UK (FAME FA41 3103 1)
Reissued in 1985 (Capitol EMS 1256)
Released in Germany on CD (EMI CDP 564-746132 2)
Current European CD (English version) (Capitol CDP 7 46474 2)

TRANS-EUROPA EXPRESS (Trans-Europe Express) (Kling Klang 06482 306)
Side One: Europa Endlos (Europe Endless), Spiegelsaal (The Hall Of Mirrors), Schaufensterpuppen (Showroom Dummies).
Side Two: Trans-Europa Express (Trans-Europe Express), Metall Auf Metall (Metal On Metal), Franz Schubert, Endlos Endlos (Endless Endless).
Early copies contained a free poster
LP released in the UK as Trans-Europe Express in different sleeve (Capitol EST 11603)
Reissued in 1985 (Fame FA 4131511)
LP released in France with Showroom Dummies in French (Les Mannequins) (Pathé-Marconi 2C068 82306)
Released in Germany on CD (Electrola CDP 564-7 461332)
Current European CD (English version) (EMI CDP 746 4732)

DIE MENSCH MASCHINE (The Man Machine) (Kling Klang 05832 843)
Side One: Die Roboter (The Robots), Spacelab, Metropolis
Side Two: Das Model (The Model), Neonlicht (Neon Lights), Die Mensch Maschine (The Man Machine).
Released in the UK as The Man Machine (Capitol EST 11728)
Reissued in 1983 (Fame FA 4131181)
Reissued in 1983 without inner sleeve (Kling Klang 05832 843)
Released in France on red vinyl.
Released in Germany on CD (Electrola 7461312)
Released in the UK on CD (Capitol CDP7 46039 2)

COMPUTERWELT (Computer World) (Kling Klang 06446 311)
Side One: Computerwelt (Computerworld), Taschenrechner (Pocket Calculator), Nummern (Numbers), Computerwelt 2 (Computerworld 2)
Side Two: Computer Liebe (Computer Love), Heimcomputer (Homecomputer), It's More Fun To Compute,
Released in the UK as Computer World (EMI EMC 3370)
Released in France with Pocket Calculator sung in French (Mini-Calculateur) (Pathé-Marconi 2C 070 64370)
Released in Japan with gatefold sleeve and insert (Toshiba EMS 91030)
Released in Germany on CD (EMI CDP 564 7 46130 2)
Released in the USA on CD (Elektra 9 3549-2)

ELECTRIC CAFE (Kling Klang 064 2406 541)
Side One: Boing Boom Tschak, Techno Pop, Musique Non Stop
Side Two: Der Telefon Anruf (The Telephone Call), Sex Objekt (Sex Object), Electric Cafe
LP released in the UK (EMI EMD 1001)
LP released in Hungary in single sleeve (Gong SLPXL 37 117)
Electric Cafe (English language version - Kling Klang 2406 441)
Electric Cafe (Edicion Español) with Sex Object sung in Spanish (EMI 074 2406881)
Released in Germany on CD (CDP 564 74 64202).
Released in the UK on CD (EMI CDP 7 464162)
Current European CD (English version) (as above)

THE MIX (Kling Klang 164-7 96650 1)
Die Roboter (The Robots), Computer Liebe (Computerlove), Taschenrechner (Pocket Calculator), Dentaku, Autobahn, Radioaktivität (Radioactivity), Trans Europa Express (Trans Europe Express), Abzug, Metall Auf Metall (Metal on Metal), Heimcomputer (Homecomputer), Music Non Stop
Released in the UK as LP (EMI EM 1408 - LP)
Released in Germany on CD (Kling Klang 568-7 96650 2)
Current European CD (English version) (EMI CDP 79 6671 2)
Released in the US on CD (Elektra 9 60869-2)

COMPILATION LPs

UK: KRAFTWERK (1&2 as a double LP)	(Vertigo 6641 077)	1972
UK: EXCELLER 8	(Vertigo 6360 629)	1975
UK: ELEKTRO KINETIK	(Vertigo 6449 066)	1981
ITALY: KRAFTWERK 1 & RALF & FLORIAN (excerpts)	(Fontana 9286 875)	
ITALY: KRAFTWERK 2 & AUTOBAHN (excerpts)	(Fontana 9286 876)	
GERMANY: DOPPELALBUM	(Philips 6623 057)	1975
GERMANY: POP LIONS (Cassette)	(Fontana 6434 348)	1976
GERMANY: HIGHRAIL (Cassette)	(Fontana 9294 124)	1979
FRANCE: AUTOBAHN (Double compilation LP)	(Philips 6623 136)	
FRANCE: KOMETENMELODIE 2 (COLLECTION A-TOUT))	(Philips 9294 803)	1976
USA: THE ROBOTS (Cassette only)	(Capitol 9445)	1986
USA: THE MODEL (RETROSPECTIVE 1975-1978)*	(Cleopatra CLEO57612)	1992

*First 1500 copies contained a colour photo from the Man Machine session and two badges and was in a black and purple bag.

German 7" Singles

Kouhoutek-Kometenmelodie 1 & 2 remix	(Philips 6003 356)	1974
Mitternacht/Morgenspaziergang/Kometenmelodie1	(Philips 6853 001)	1974
Autobahn/Morgenspaziergang	(Philips 6003 438)	1974
Kometenmelodie 2/Mitternacht	(Philips 6003 466)	1975
Autobahn/Kometenmelodie 2 (re-issue)	(Vertigo 6147 012)	1976
Radioaktivität/Antenne	(Kling Klang 82119)	1976
Trans Europa Express/Franz Schubert	(Kling Klang 85077)	1977
Die Roboter/Spacelab	(Kling Klang 32941)	1978

Die Roboter/Spacelab (red vinyl)	(Kling Klang 32941)	1978
Das Model/Neonlicht	(Kling Klang 45109)	1978
Taschenrechner/Dentaku	(EMI 46365)	1981
Das Model/The Model	(Kling Klang 78078)	1982
Tour De France(German version)		
/Tour De France (French version)	(EMI 1652047)	1983
Tour De France (remix)/Tour De France (instrumental)	(EMI 200376)	1984
Musique Non Stop/Musique Non Stop (version)	(EMI 2015087)	1986
Der Telefon Anruf (remix)/The Telephone Call (remix)	(EMI 2016327)	1987
Die Roboter (single edit)/Robotronik (single edit)	(Electrola 006 2043257)	1991
Radioaktivität (Francois Kevorkian remix)/		
Radioaktivität (William Orbit remix)	(EMI 2045167)	1991

German 12" singles

Die Roboter/Das Model/Neonlicht/T.E.E.	(Kling Klang 45176)	1978
Die Roboter/Das Model/Neonlicht/T.E.E.(red vinyl)	(Kling Klang 45176)	1978
Computerwelt (remix)/Nummern/Computerwelt 2	(EMI 46379)	1981
Das Model/The Model	(Klling Klang 78078)	1982
Tour De France (German version)/		
Tour De France (French version)	(EMI 1652046)	1983
Tour De France (Francois Kevorkian remix)/		
Tour De France (version)/ Tour De France (7" version)	(EMI 2003776)	1984
Musique Non Stop/Musique Non Stop (7" version)	(EMI 2015236)	1986
Der Telefon Anruf/Housephone/Telephone Call	(EMI 2016336)	1987
Robotnik/Die Roboter (single edit)/Robotronik*	(EMI 2043256)	1991
Radioactivity (Francois Kevorkian 12" remix)/		
Radioactivitat (Francois Kevorkian 7" remix)/		
Radioactivitat (William Orbit 12" remix)*	(EMI 2045166)	1991
* also available as CD singles		

UK 7" Singles

Autobahn/Kometenmelodie 1	(Vertigo 6147 012)	1975
Comet Melody 2/Kristallo	(Vertigo 6147 015)	1975
Radioactivity/Antenna	(Capitol CL 15853)	1976
Trans Europe Express/Europe Endless	(Capitol CL 15917)	1977
Showroom Dummies/Europe Endless	(Capitol CLX 104)	1977
The Robots/Spacelab (fold out picture cover)	(Capitol CL 15981)	1978
The Robots/Spacelab (alternate mix)	(Capitol CL 15981)	1978
Neonlights/T.E.E./The Model	(Capitol CL 15998)	1978
Autobahn/ *Classical Gas by Beggars Opera*	(Vertigo CUT 108)	1981
Pocket Calculator/Dentaku	(EMI 5175)	1981
Computer Love/The Model	(EMI 5207)	1981
Kometenmelodie 2/Vom Himmel Hoch	(Vertigo VER 3)	1981
The Model/Computer Love (different sleeve)	(EMI 5207)	1981
Showroom Dummies (edit) /Numbers(remix)	(EMI 5272)	1982
Tour De France/Tour De France (instrumental)	(EMI 5413)	1983
Computer Love/The Model (reissue)	(EMI G45 16)	1984
Tour De France (remix)/Tour De France	(EMI 5413)	1984
Musique Non Stop/Musique Non Stop (version)	(EMI 5588)	1986
The Telephone Call/Der Telefon Anruf	(EMI 5602)	1987
The Robots (remix)/Robotronik (single version)	(EM 192)	1991
The Robots (remix)/Robotronik (single version)	(EM 192) dif sleeve	1991
Radioactivity (Francois Kevorkian 7" remix)/		
Radioactivity (William Orbit 7" remix)	(EM 201)	1991

UK 12" Singles

Showroom Dummies/Europe Endless	(Capitol 12 CLX 104)	1978
Showroom Dummies/Europe Endless/Spacelab	(Capitol CL 16098)	1978
Neonlights/T.E.E./The Model (luminous vinyl)	(Capitol CL 15998)	1978
Pocket Calculator/Numbers/Dentaku	(EMI 12 EMI 5175)	1981
Computer Love/The Model	(EMI 12 EMI 5207)	1981
The Model/Computer Love	(EMI 12 EMI 5207)	1981
Showroom Dummies/Numbers/Pocket Calculator	(EMI 12 EMI 5272)	1981
Tour De France (long version)/Tour De France (7")/		
Tour De France (2e Étape)	(EMI 12 EMI 5413)	1983
Tour De France (Francois Kevorkian remix)		
/Tour De France (version)/ Tour De France (7")	(EMI 12 EMI 5413)	1984
Musique Non Stop/Musique Non Stop (7" version)	(EMI 12 EMI 5588)	1986

The Telephone Call/Der Telefon Anruf/Housephone	(EMI 12 EMI 5602)	1987
Robotronik/The Robots (single edit)/ The Robots	(12 EM 192)	1991
Robotronik/The Robots (single edit)/The Robots	(12 EM 192) dif sleeve	1991
Radioactivity (Francois Kevorkian 12" remix)/		
Radioactivity (Francois Kevorkian 7" remix)/		
Radioactivity (William Orbit 12" remix)	(12EM 201/2045526))	1991

UK Cassette Singles

Pocket Calculator (long version)/Numbers/Dentaku	(EMI TC EMI 5175)	1981
Tour De France/Tour de France (version)		
Tour De France (2 Étape) all 3 tracks on both sides	(EMI TC EMI 5413)	1983
The Robots/Robotnik	(EMI TC EM 192)	1991
The Robots/Robotnik (different sleeve)	(EMI TC EM 192)	1991
Radioactivity (Francois Kevorkian 12" remix)		
/Radioactivity (William Orbit 7" remix)	(EMI TC EM 201)	1991

UK CD Singles

Robotronik/Robotnik/Robotronik (single version)	(CD EM 192)	1991
Robotronik/Robotnik/The Robots (different sleeve)	(CD EM 192)	1991
Radioactivity (Francois Kevorkian 7" &12" remixes)		
/Radioactivity (William Orbit 12" remix)	(CD EM 2012045522)	1991

USA 7" singles

Autobahn (edit)/Morgenspaziergang	(Vertigo VE203)
Kometenmelodie 2 (edit)/Mitternacht	(Vertigo VE204)
Radioactivity(edit)/Antenna (edit)	(Capitol 4211)
Trans-Europe Express/Franz Schubert	(Capitol 4460)
Showroom Dummies/Les Mannequins	(Capitol 8502)
The Robots (edit)/Neon Lights (edit)	(Capitol 4620)
Pocket Calculator (edit)/Dentaku (edit) Yellow vinyl	(WBS 49723)
Computer Love (edit)/ Numbers (edit)	(WBS 49795)
Musique Non Stop/Musique Non Stop	(WBS 7-28532)
The Telephone Call (remix)/Der Telefon Anruf	(WBS7-28441)

USA 12" and CD single releases

Trans-Europe Express/Franz Schubert	(Capitol 8513)
Showroom Dummies/Les Mannequins	(Capitol 8502)
Tour De France (French version)/Tour De France (remix)	(WBS 20146-0)
Musique Non Stop/Musique Non Stop 7"	(WBS 7599 20549)
The Telephone Call (remix)/Housephone/	
Der Telefon Anruf	(WBS 7599 20627)
The Robots/Neon Lights/Trans Europe Express/	
Showroom Dummies 12" (Kraftwerk's Disco Best EP)	(Capitol 8865/8866)
Trans-Europe Express/Trans-Europe Express (edit)/	
Les Mannequins/Showroom Dummies	(Capitol CD C2-15620)
Robotnik (Kling Klang Mix)/The Robots (single edit)/	
Robotronik (Kling Klang mix) 12"	(Elektra 0-66526)
The Robots(single edit)/Robotnik (Kling Klang mix)/	
Robotronik (Kling Klang mix) CD single	(Elektra 9 66526-2
The Robots(single edit)/Robotnik (Kling Klang mix)	(Elektra PRCD8392-2)
Radioactivity (Francois Kevorkian 12" remix)/	
Radiocativity (LP Version)/	
Radiocativity (William Orbit Hardcore Mix)/	
Radioactivity (William Orbit 12" remix) 12"	(Elecktra 0-66486)
Showroom Dummies (CD single)	(CLEO 6843)

Japanese 7" singles

The Model/Computer Love (edit)	(EMI EMS 17223)
The Robots (edit)/Trans Europe Express (edit)	(Capitol ECR 20476
Showroom Dummies/The Robots	(Capitol ECR 20658)
Dentaku (edit)/ Pocket Calculator (edit)	(EMI EMS 17145)

Spanish 7" singles

Autobahn (edit)/Morgenspaziergang	(Vertigo 6147 009)
Radioactividad (edit)/Antenna (edit)	(Capitol 1J 006-82.119)
Showroom Dummies/The Hall of Mirrors	(Capitol 10C 006-085.211)
The Robots (edit)/Spacelab (edit)	(Capitol 10C-006-085.496)
The Model/Computer Love (edit)	(EMI 10C 006 064509)
The Model/Metropolis (edit)	(Capitol 10C 006-085965)

Belgian 7" singles
Radioactivity (edit)/Antenna (edit)   (Capitol 4C 010-82119)
The Robots (edit)/Spacelab (edit)   (Capitol 4C 006 85496)

Portuguese 7" singles
Pocket Calculator (edit)/Dentaku (edit)   (EMI 11C008 64365H)
The Model/Computer Love   (EMI 11C 008 64509)

Irish 7" singles
The Model/Computer Love   (EMI 5207)

Canadian 7"/12" singles
Autobahn (edit)/Morning Walk 7"   (Vertigo VE203)
Trans-Europe Express/*The BB&Q Band "On The Beat"* 12"   (Unidisc SPEC1373)

Italian 7" singles
Radioactivity (edit)/Antenna (edit)   (EMI 3C 006-82119)
Trans-Europe Express (edit)/Franz Schubert   (Capitol 3C 006-85077)
The Robots (edit)/Spacelab (edit)   (Capitol 3C 006 85496)
The Model/Computer Love (edit)   (EMI 3C-008-64509)
Pocket Calculator (edit)/Dentaku (edit)   (EMI 3C 006-64365)
Musique Non Stop (7" version)/Musique Non Stop (version)   (EMI 06-2015087)

French 7"/12" singles
Radioactivity(edit)/ Antenna (edit)   (Capitol 2C 010-82119)
Trans-Europe Express (edit)/Franz Schubert   (Capitol 2C 006-85077)
Les Mannequins (edit)/The Hall of Mirrors   (Capitol 2C 006 85211)
The Robots (edit)/Spacelab (edit)   (Capitol 2S 008 85496)
The Model/Computer Love (edit)   (EMI 2C-008-64509)
Tour De France/Tour De France (instrumental)   (Pathé-Marconi 1651867)
Tour De France (New York Club mix/ French)/
Tour De France (New York Club mix/German 12"   (Pathé-Marconi 1545236)
Musique Non-Stop/Musique Non Stop (version)   (Pathé-Marconi 2015087)

Dutch 7" singles
Radioactivity (edit)/Antenna (edit)   (Capitol 5C 006-82119)
The Model/The Man Machine   (Capitol 5C-006-85673)
The Model/Computer Love (edit)   (EMI 1A-006-64509)
The Robots (edit)/Spacelab (edit)   (Capitol 5C 006 85496)
The Telephone Call (Remix edit)/Der Telefon Anruf   (EMI 1A-006 20.16377)

Brazilian 7" singles
The Robots/Spacelab/The Model/Neon Lights   (Capitol 31C 016 85870)

Argentinian 7" singles
Europe Endless (part 1)/Europe Endless (part 2)   (Capitol EP 2483)
Europe Endless (part 1)/The Hall of Mirrors   (Capitol 101042)
Metropolis (edit)/The Model   (Capitol FAN-S/23/101 072)
Computer World (part 1)/Computer Love (edit)   (EMI 7SCR/F3959/1787)

Australian 7" singles
The Robots (single edit)/Robotronik   (EMI MX 78462)
The Model/Computer Love (edit)   (EMI 675)

Video
Frontiers of Progressive Rock No 7.
Kraftwerk track "Truckstop Gondelero"   Laserdisc/Pioneer SM 048-3227

THE ONE AND ONLY: Peter Perrett - Homme Fatale by Nina Antonia
ISBN: 0946 719 16 0.
224 pages (illustrated). £11.95
An extraordinary journey through crime, punishment and the decadent times of The Only Ones. Includes interviews with Perrett and all ex-band members.
"Antonia gets everyone's co-operation and never loses her perspective on Perrett". **Mojo.**
"Antonia is the ideal chronicler of Perrett's rise and fall. From his time as drug dealer, to the smack sojourn in The Only Ones, Perrett's tale is one of self-abuse and staggering selfishness". **Select**

Plunderphonics, 'Pataphysics and Pop Mechanics by Andrew Jones
ISBN: 0946 719 15 2.
256 pages (illustrated). £12.95
Chris Cutler, Fred Frith, Henry Threadgill, Ferdinand Richard, Amy Denio, Lindsay Cooper, John Oswald, John Zorn, The Residents and many more....
"The talent assembled between Jones's covers would be interesting under any rubric. Thought provoking and stimulating". **Mojo**
"Jones's book is perhaps the first study of the growth of these techniques within the avant-garde. Packed with fascinating interviews and written with wit and insight". **Q magazine**

Dark Entries - Bauhaus and Beyond by Ian Shirley
ISBN: 0946 719 13 6.
200 pages (illustrated). £11.95
The full gothic rise and fall of Bauhaus, including offshoot projects, Love and Rockets, Tones on Tail, Daniel Ash, David J and Peter Murphy. Ian Shirley unravels the uncompromising story of four individuals who have consistently confounded their detractors by turning up the unexpected.
"A trench-to-toilet missive of who did what, where and when. It works brilliantly". **Alternative Press.**
"Solidly researched account of goth-tinged glam". **Top magazine.**

Wrong Movements - A Robert Wyatt History by Mike King
ISBN: 0946 719 10 1.
160 pages (illustrated). £14.95
A sumptuous and detailed journey through Robert Wyatt's 30 year career with Soft Machine, Matching Mole and as a highly respected solo artist. Packed with previously unpublished archive material and rare photos. Commentary from Wyatt himself, Hugh Hopper, Mike Ratledge, Daevid Allen, Kevin Ayers & more.
"King's careful chronology and Wyatt's supreme modesty produce a marvellously unhysterical, oddly haunting book". **Q magazine**
"Low key, likeable and lefty. Like the man himself". **iD magazine**

No More Mr. Nice Guy - The Inside Story of the Alice Cooper Group by original guitarist Michael Bruce and Billy James
ISBN: 0946 719 17 9.   160 pages (illustrated). £9.95
Michael Bruce opens the lid on his years with the platinum selling group, revealing the truth behind the publicity stunts, the dead babies, the drinking, the executions and, of course, the rock 'n' roll.
"I'm Eighteen changed Alice Cooper from the group that destroyed chickens to the group that destroyed stadiums". **Village Voice.**
"It might even be argued that the band defined what it meant to be a role ridden seventies teenager". **Rolling Stone**

Wire - Everybody Loves a History by Kevin Eden
ISBN: 0946 719 07 1.
192 pages (illustrated). £9.95
A fascinating look at one of punk's most endearing and enduring bands, including interviews with all band members. A self-analysis of the complex motivations which have often seen the various members cross the boundaries between music and art.
"Any band or their fans could feel well served by a book like Eden's". **Vox**
"Eden delivers a sharp portrayal of the punk industry's behaviour, influence and morality". **Q magazine**

TAPE DELAY by Charles Neal
ISBN: 0946 719 02 0.
256 pages (illustrated). £11.95
Marc Almond, Cabaret Voltaire, Nick Cave, Chris & Cosey, Coil, Foetus, Neubauten, Non, The Fall, The The, Lydia Lunch, New Order, Psychic TV, Rollins, Sonic Youth, Swans, Test Department and many more...
"A virtual Who's Who of people who've done the most to drag music out of commercial confinement". **NME.**
"Intriguing and interesting". **Q magazine.**

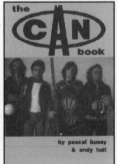

THE CAN BOOK by Pascal Bussy
ISBN: 0946 719 05 5.
192 pages (illustrated). £8.95
A complete histoy of Krautrock supremos, including band member biographies, chronology and discography.
"If Can's music is a mystery, then this book will make you want to investigate further". **Q magazine**
"Bussy's account of the characters and chronology of Can is helpfully musicalogical for the fan and iced generously enough with information and anecdotes to attract the as yet unaligned". **Melody Maker**

About the author:
Pascal Bussy lives in Paris with his wife and two children. He is also the author of The Can Book (published by SAF) as well as several books about wine. At one time he ran his own label which released music by Can, This Heat, Eyeless In Gaza and Lol Coxhill amongst others. He is currently head of the jazz department of Warners in Paris.

FORTHCOMING TITLES:

DIGITAL GOTHIC: A critical history of Tangerine Dream by Paul Stump. Due Spring '97

BOOK TRADE DISTRIBUTION
UK & EUROPE:
Airlift Book Company, 8 The Arena, Mollison Ave, Enfield, Middx. EN3 7NJ.
Tel: 0181 804 0400 Fax: 0181 804 0044
USA:
Last Gasp, 777 Florida Street, San Francisco, CA94110.
Tel: 415 824 6636 Fax: 415 824 1836
Canada:
Marginal Distribution, Unit 102, 277 George Street North, Peterborough, Ontario, Canada. K9J 3G9.
Tel/Fax: 705 745 2326

Titles also available through: Caroline Export, Lasgo Export, Firebird (USA), See Hear (USA), Wayside Music (USA) Virgin Records, Tower Records and all good bookshops.
If you find difficulty obtaining any title, all SAF books are stocked and available mail order from:
Helter Skelter Bookshop, 4 Denmark Street, London WC2H 8LL Tel: 0171 836 1151 Fax: 0171 240 9880.

SAF Publishing Ltd

12 Conway Gardens, Wembley, Middx. HA9 8TR. England
Tel: +44 (0)181 904 6263 Fax: +44 (0)181 930 8565